Royal City

Heritage
House

VICTORIA • VANCOUVER • CALGARY

JIM WOLF

Royal City

1858–1960

A Photographic History of New Westminster

Heritage House Publishing Company Ltd.
#108–17665 66a Avenue
Surrey, BC V3S 2A7
www.heritagehouse.ca

Library and Archives Canada Cataloguing in Publication
Wolf, Jim
  Royal city: a photographic history of New Westminster, 1858–1960 / Jim Wolf.

Includes bibliographical references and index.

ISBN 1-894384-84-9 (hardcover)
ISBN 1-894384-97-0 (softcover)

    1. New Westminster (B.C.)—Pictorial works. 2. New Westminster (B.C.)
—History. 3. Photographers—British Columbia—New Westminster—Biography.
4. New Westminster (B.C.)—Biography. I. Title.

FC3849.N49W64 2005   971.1'33   C2005-905947-8

Edited by Marial Shea
Cover and book design by Frances Hunter

Printed in Canada

Heritage House acknowledges the financial support for its publishing program from
the Government of Canada through the Book Publishing Industry Development
Program (BPIDP), Canada Council for the Arts, and the British Columbia Arts Council.

The Canada Council | Le Conseil des Arts
for the Arts | du Canada

BRITISH COLUMBIA
ARTS COUNCIL
We acknowledge the support of the Province of British Columbia
through the British Columbia Arts Council

Contents

Pages 2–3: *The site of the colonial capital of New Westminster had been transformed from a primeval forest into an important settlement in just seven years when it was captured in this magical panorama.*

F.G. CLAUDET PHOTOGRAPH, C. 1866. IHP 0618.

ACKNOWLEDGEMENTS

This project took shape slowly over a number of years of personal research, but was pulled together in just a few short months with the help of so many. It could never have been possible without the contributions of some incredible individuals dedicated to the preservation of the Royal City's heritage. The overwhelming support and assistance I received in initiating and completing this book project was another affirmation of the tremendous spirit of this community.

I am personally indebted to the members and the board of directors of the New Westminster Heritage Preservation Society and Arts Council of New Westminster, who gave me their confidence and provided the core of the project's research funding. This book would never have been possible without the personal efforts of Ethel Field, one of this city's great ladies, who led the book committee with such professionalism and wit. The board of the Arts Council, especially Hilda Cliff and Andrée St. Martin, deserve credit for providing unwavering support to the project when funding was critical.

This project is also the result of the foresight shown by the City of New Westminster, which established the perpetual Heritage Endowment Grant Program. I am very grateful to all of the city's dedicated and professional staff and wish to especially thank Cultural Services Coordinator Colleen Gould and Assistant Director of Planning Leslie Gilbert for shepherding the project to its final approval by the grant committee and city council.

No book on the history of the city could be written without utilizing the collections of the New Westminster Museum and Archives amassed by those dedicated curators that were committed to preserving photographs and documents on behalf of the community. I am grateful to former museum manager Valerie Francis for hiring me 20 years ago to organize the archives, an experience that inspired me to write this book. On my most recent return to the New Westminster Museum and Archives as a researcher, a new generation of staff put up with my early morning visits and numerous archival requests with so much professionalism and support. Thanks are extended to Jacqueline O'Donnell, Diane Thorpe, Jason Haight, Ellen Willet and all of the staff and volunteers. I owe a special thank you to the newly hired and very talented archivist, Kelly Stewart, who allowed me to dig deep into boxes of unaccessioned materials to recover "lost gems." Allan Blair can be credited for his expert scanning of the photographs in the museum's collection. My friend and graphic designer Rod Nevison also provided his talents to scan images and piece together panoramic views.

I am so fortunate to have been able to use the collection of the New Westminster Public Library. Although long retired, chief librarian Alan Woodland and reference librarian Joss Halverson contributed so much to this institution's outstanding local history collection. All of the librarians of the reference department staff put up with my innumerable requests to answer the most obscure historical questions and find almost anything. I especially wish to thank Wendy Turnbull and Ann Lunghamer for their assistance with this project.

David Mattison, Royal B.C. Museum archivist and historian emeritus of B.C. photographers, provided much assistance and inspiration. I am grateful for his kind permission to use his Camera Workers research as a basis for this book's appendix of photographers.

At Heritage House I am indebted to the entire team, but especially wish to thank Rodger Touchie for taking on this project; Vivian Sinclair for managing everything; Marial Shea for her expert editing; and Frances Hunter for designing a beautiful book.

And last on the list, but always first in my life, I wish to thank and acknowledge my family. My best friend and partner Lauren inspired me to keep writing, despite having to suffer many weekends as a "book widow." I owe thanks to my son Griffin, a true native of the Royal City, for giving me time to play and enjoy the places that make this city so special. To them I dedicate this book.

Foreword

For Vancouverites like me, a child in the 1950s, New Westminster was the place you passed through on the way to the Pattullo Bridge and thence the Trans Canada Highway, a.k.a. the Fraser Highway. Had we stopped at this first capital of the colony of British Columbia, we would have found a gracious and prosperous industrial city and transportation hub. To the people in the agricultural Fraser Valley, it was their bright lights, their market-town destination.

Then, in the late '50s, the opening of the Massey tunnel between Richmond and Delta and the completion of Highway 99 made it possible to get to the Fraser Valley and beyond without passing through "New West" at all. In 1964, the opening of the Port Mann Bridge and the completion of the freeway to Vancouver's doorstep dealt New Westminster the coup de grace. Or so it seemed. Thereafter, to us outsiders, it was "genteel shabby"—old loggers in the beer parlours on Columbia Street, CKNW radio, the BC Pen on the hillside above the Fraser and some quiet residential streets near Queen's Park. New Westminster seemed caught in the past while the rest of the Lower Mainland flung itself headlong into the maelstrom of malls, cars and skyscrapers.

In retrospect, the events of the '50s and '60s bought the Royal City some time, allowing the attitudes of its residents to catch up with the remarkable historical legacy left from the nineteenth and early twentieth centuries. A slow economy and little change meant that much of the city's glorious architecture escaped the redevelopment crunch. These period streetscapes give context to Jim Wolf's book, raising it well above the level of mere nostalgia. His research adds layers of history onto a modern city that hasn't wilfully discarded its roots. There is magic in the old photographs, a through-the-looking-glass journey into a world eerily like our own, yet so different in manners and mobility.

Jim Wolf is part of the tradition of historically aware, activist New Westminster residents who are stewards of the community's past and cornerstones of its future. But his knowledge is much deeper than most: for 20 years he has connected the dots between architects, photographers, almost-forgotten citizens and the streets of his beloved city. In this book, he bridges the gap between the familiar places of the modern city and their early years, giving us a tour through New Westminster's richly textured past.

Michael Kluckner

Introduction

FROM ITS VERY BEGINNING, New Westminster has been blessed with some incredibly talented resident photographers who viewed our city with expert eyes, capturing history in magical moments with the click of their cameras. This book celebrates the skill and artistry of these photographers, bringing their names and their work forward to receive the recognition they deserve. Along with the photographs, this book provides a brief biography of some of the Royal City's best-known professional and amateur photographers. An appendix is included to identify all of the names and operational dates of the many other prominent Royal City-based studio photographers who left their own legacy of unforgettable images.

Along with photographers, we also owe a great debt to the city's early writers. It was the reporters and editors of our hometown newspapers, especially those working for *The British Columbian*, who documented the soul of our city with their words; they will forever be part of our collective heritage. Presenting this photographic history of New Westminster without historical context would have been impossible. However brief, the accompanying overview of our city's tumultuous times incorporates the words of those who witnessed and recorded these events. Often, a witness's written description creates an even more vivid picture of events, adding to the drama of these extraordinary photographs.

In 1985, I was an eager university student who had just landed a summer job at New Westminster's Irving House Historic Centre, cataloguing a collection of historic photographs. There seemed to be no end to the stacks of dusty images and albums needing care and attention. Wearing white gloves to protect the photographs, I adopted the almost scientific pose of an archivist. I began to neatly number and identify each treasure one by one, carefully placing each amazingly fragile piece of emulsified paper into a stark white, acid-free envelope.

The idea of compiling a book filled with photographs took shape during that fateful summer. Over 20 years later, my obsession with the city's early history and photographs continues. Even after all these years, I cannot manage to restrain the joy of seeing, for the first time, a new rare image of some forgotten time and place that was the Royal City. This book is an attempt to recapture our city's remarkable history through surviving historic photographs, many of which have never been published before. These photographic artifacts have survived an almost miraculous journey, from the moment of their creation through a photographer's lens, to possession as treasure, then often surviving neglect and indifference, and on to the final momentous deposit as a new addition to the archives.

In a sense, this book has really been in the making for more than 100 years. After all, it would not have been possible to compile this work without the artistry and skill of the city's early photographers and the dedication of some remarkable citizens, historians, institutions and their staff in creating, preserving and sharing these documents.

As I discovered the pieces to this book in the archival collections of the Irving House Historic Centre and the New Westminster Public Library, I could not help but appreciate the foresight and dedication of the city's earliest historians, archivists and librarians, who established these institutions to gather and preserve the historic record of this place and its people. Our library, founded in 1865, is the oldest civic institution of its kind in western Canada, and was the first to preserve valued books and documents. The New Westminster Art, Historical and Scientific Association, formed by culturally minded residents in 1895, even used the civic library to open the first museum in the city. Although it was tragically destroyed by the Great Fire of 1898, the library was eventually rebuilt, and its democratic principles have ensured that this civic collection has been available to the general public ever since.

The early establishment of the New Westminster branch of the Native Sons of B.C. Post #4 in 1908 promised the beginning of a grass-roots community effort to preserve our documentary heritage. The Native Sons had a few dedicated historians, including Judge F.W. Howay and "Ernie" Cotton. But the majority of the boys appeared to have been more interested in getting together for "smokers" than getting anything tangible in terms of an archives accomplished. It was thanks to the city's history-minded women, who in 1924 formed the Native Daughters of B.C. Post #4, that real progress towards a historic centre finally began. Not only did these ladies open the first museum and archives in 1927, they also began their steadfast effort to preserve Irving House. Their lobbying finally accomplished this incredible feat with the help of the Native Sons when the "city's oldest house" was purchased by the city in 1950. Despite the biases often shown by these early collectors as to what constituted the history of our city, the collections they gathered have provided an invaluable resource and legacy.

Through these photographs, the New Westminster of the past lives again. Take a walk down dusty streets and explore mysterious buildings, disasters and celebrations of long ago. In combining historic descriptions of places and events with the identification of persons, the viewing of a photograph can become more intense. Even viewing numerous anonymous portraits taken in a photographer's studio becomes intimate as each prop and piece of furnishing, at first meaningless, becomes familiar—a point of identification of its place and time. The moment your memory connects one piece of information to another is magical. Suddenly, an unidentified photograph of a place or person is rediscovered and "remembered." Just so, the information reaped from viewing and describing hundreds of photographic images slowly began to rebuild a lost city in my mind as the connections of history, people and events came together. It is my hope that you experience this same magic as you explore the text and images in these pages.

Here, in modern-day New Westminster, I am always reminded how much we, its citizens, owe to the history of this place. The vision and excellent planning of Colonel Moody left us with a city that is eminently livable because of its outstanding urban design and careful preservation of parks. Many of us occupy the beautiful homes of earlier generations and walk on century-old sidewalks. We are still so fortunate to have the opportunity to relive our history and celebrate the ever-resilient spirit of our community in the celebrations of May Day and Victoria Day. Weaving together images and memories, this book celebrates the collective history that makes the Royal City such a special place in our hearts and minds.

CHAPTER 1

1858–1868

The Imperial Stumpfield

Previous page: *The Royal Engineers' camp was carved out of the woods to create a village quite separate from the town. Government House at left was built in 1861 and served as the residence of Colonel Moody and his family. On occasional visits to the mainland, Governor Douglas insisted on residing here, which Mary Moody regarded as a "nuisance."*

F.G. CLAUDET PHOTOGRAPH, C. 1862. IHP 0623

he remarkable site of our city was once a sublimely beautiful wilderness that, for thousands of years, was home to the Sto:lo (river) people. This location remains an essential part of the proud oral history and culture of the Sto:lo. Their name for New Westminster is "Sxwaymelth," after a legendary warrior who was turned to stone by the transformer Xexa:ls. The "Sxwaymelth" stone was believed to contain the "shxweli" (life force) of that ancient ancestral warrior who gave this location great power. This revered stone landmark was once located prominently on the river bank of our city.

The Qw'ó:ntl'an (Kwantlen, meaning noble or high born) were one of the ancient tribes of the Sto:lo and have always claimed the site of New Westminster as their ancestral home. It is said that, at the beginning of time, the transformer turned the original people living here into wolves and sent them into the woods, giving this land to the Qw'ó:ntl'an. The names of several village and food-gathering locations have been recorded and serve to illustrate the connection of the Sto:lo people to this land. On the lower banks of "Scuwiheya" (now Burnaby Lake and the Brunette River) was "Tsítslhes," a place for wind-drying fish. Nearby was the large Qw'ó:ntl'an village of "Skwekwte'xwqen" (which became the site of the Royal Engineers' Camp), and beside the Stótelö (Glen Brook) were places named "Statelew" and "Schechi:les" (strong lungs). It was here on the high banks above the river that the wooden boxes containing the bones of ancestors would be placed in trees and inside hollows under roots. Immediately across the river was the village of "Qayqayt" (resting place), a small seasonal fishing and hunting location and a place to pick "qwemchó:ls"(cranberries) during the fall.

The first known contact of Aboriginal peoples with Europeans occurred in the late 1700s through trading with the earliest explorers and fur traders sailing along the coast of North America. The first European account of the river valley was written in 1808. Simon Fraser, a partner in the North West Company, was intent on exploring the country west of the Rocky Mountains. He descended the upper reaches of what he thought was the Columbia River to find its route to the Pacific. Instead, he discovered that his chosen river was not the Columbia, but a treacherous waterway with deep canyons, part of the territory of local native people hostile to his presence. As Fraser moved down the river valley, he was met with increased hostility from local chiefs and warriors as he refused to follow their protocols. At the village of Musqueam, the party arrived without due and proper respect and were considered enemies. Warriors "began to make their appearance from every direction howling like so many wolves, brandishing their war clubs." Fraser and his crew had to abandon their expedition and desperately paddle back up the river. They were eventually able to escape with their lives.

The initial contact with European trading expeditions had devastating results for Aboriginal people, as many contracted and died from the diseases brought by the traders. Smallpox became such an epidemic in the river valley in 1782 that it is believed as many as one-third of the Sto:lo people died. It was the Hudson's Bay Company that finally moved into the lower Fraser River to trade with the Sto:lo peoples and build Fort Langley in 1827. The Qw'ó:ntl'an eventually all but abandoned their village sites on the lower river to move nearer the fort and reap the benefits of being the local native group in control of access to the fur traders. They became more or less like agents or dealers,

The Sto:lo were ever-present in the early days of New Westminster's development and adapted quickly to new customs, including wearing western clothing. These men and women were photographed at a religious gathering organized by the Oblates of Mary Immaculate.

F. DALLY PHOTOGRAPHER, C.1868. NWPL 1416

New Westminster's founder, Colonel Richard Clement Moody (1813–1887), poses confidently in his fine military uniform of the Royal Engineers.

F. DALLY PHOTOGRAPH, C. 1860. NWPL 623

rather than hunters and trappers, serving as middlemen between other Natives and the Hudson's Bay Company, controlling its fur trade.

The Fort also provided protection for local Aboriginal people from Kwagiulth warriors. These warriors would travel from their village of Yuculta (now known as Cape Mudge, Quadra Island) to attack Sto:lo villages, killing men and abducting women and children for slaves. Fur traders realized that warfare among the Natives interfered with their ability to conduct business. In 1837 Fort Langley was the scene of a bloody battle between 25 fur traders and a Kwagiulth war party of 600 sent to attack the Sto:lo people. The use of cannons fired from the protective bastions of the fort quickly resulted in a massacre of the Kwagiulth warriors and put an end to further raids.

Discovery of gold in British Columbia in 1857 changed the destiny of this isolated outpost of the British Empire. The news reached California and the stampede of thousands of American gold miners began. James Douglas, the Hudson's Bay Company's Chief Factor and governor of the colony of Vancouver Island, sent warnings to London, fearing an American annexation of the territory. The correspondence was received by Colonial Secretary Sir Edward Bulwer-Lytton, who had been at work in this new cabinet post for only three weeks. Bulwer-Lytton immediately introduced the bill creating the new colony of British Columbia on August 2, 1858, and appointed Douglas as governor.

Alarmed by the threat posed by the possible American control of the Fraser River goldfields and the lack of British forces on the coast, Bulwer-Lytton decided that a corps of sappers and miners would be formed as the Columbia Detachment of Royal Engineers. The War Office selected Colonel Richard Clement Moody, the former governor of the Falkland Islands and the commander of the Royal Engineers at Edinburgh. Moody accepted the appointment as commander of the Columbia Detachment of Royal Engineers and was also awarded the offices of Chief Commissioner of Lands and Works and Lieutenant-Governor of British Columbia.

The first contingent of Royal Engineers, led by Captain Parsons, left on its long ocean voyage on September 2, 1858, from Southhampton. Bulwer-Lytton addressed the first group of men from the dock: "Soldiers—I have come to say to you a few kind words of parting. You are going to a distant country, not, I trust, to fight against men, but to conquer nature; not to besiege cities, but to create them; not to overthrow kingdoms but to assist in establishing new communications under the scepter of your own Queen. For these noble objects, you soldiers of the Royal Engineers have been especially selected from the ranks of Her Majesty's armies. The enterprise before you is indeed glorious. Ages hence industry and commerce will crowd the roads that you will have made ... [and] ... dwell in the cities of which you will map the sites and lay the foundations." [1]

Top: *It was from the deck of the* Beaver *that Colonel Moody spotted the future site of New Westminster on January 5, 1859. Moody was on his first trip up the Fraser River.*

PHOTOGRAPHER UNKNOWN, C.1871. IHP

Bottom: *Governor James Douglas was despised in New Westminster for blatantly undermining the city's economy with proclamations that favoured the economy of Victoria.*

PHOTOGRAPHER UNKNOWN, C. 1860. AUTHOR'S COLLECTION.

The first contingent of Royal Engineers arrived on October 29, 1858. Captain Parsons and 20 men, mainly surveyors, were just in time to witness the reading of the proclamation at Fort Langley on November 19, 1858, creating the new colony. Governor Douglas had also made a rather startling and self-serving decision prior to the arrival of the Royal Engineers. He ordered Vancouver Island's Colonial Surveyor, J.D. Pemberton, to survey a 900-acre new town named Derby at the site of the first Fort Langley. Here he had evicted some land speculators from Victoria who were squatting in the hope that they could claim the site for a town. This site was conspicuously adjacent to the Hudson's Bay Company's extensive land holdings. Although Douglas had issued no proclamation, he had done everything to create the impression that Derby would become the new capital city and had even started the construction of new barracks here for the reception of the Royal Engineers. Prominent businessmen of Vancouver Island, many of them old friends of Douglas, were eager to gain a potential lucrative investment, and spent over 13,000 pounds purchasing lots at an auction held in Victoria on November 25, 1858.

Colonel Moody arrived in Victoria, the capital of the colony of Vancouver Island, with his wife Mary and their four children on Christmas Day, December 25, 1858. After a brief rest, Moody boarded the *Beaver* and steamed to the new colony of British Columbia on January 5, 1859. Travelling up the main channel of the Fraser River, Moody was immediately struck by the perfection of a site at the fork of the river's delta as the location for a great city. He recorded his observations in a letter to his friend Arthur Blackwood of the Colonial Office:

> The entrance to the Fraser River is very striking. Extending miles to the right and to the left, are low marsh lands and yet from the background of superb mountains, Swiss in outline, dark in woods grandly towering into the clouds, there is a sublimity that deeply impresses you. Everything is large and magnificent! I scarcely ever enjoyed a scene so much in my life! My imagination converted the silent marshes … [into] … pictures of horses and cattle lazily fattening in the rich meadows in a glowing sunset. One cannot write prosaically of such scenes as these, so pray make allowances when I get into rhapsodies at any time about this most beautiful country.
>
> The water of the deep clear Frazer [sic] was of a glassy stillness—not a ripple before us except when a fish rose to the surface, or broods of wild ducks fluttered away. Soon we reached the woodland district. The contrast with the treeless meadows just past was very striking!
>
> In steaming up one fine reach at a spot 20 miles from the entrance to the channel of the Fraser, my attention was at once arrested by its fitness in all probability for a site of the first, if not the Chief Town, in the country.
>
> Further study of that ground, as well as other sites, has now convinced me that IT is the right place in all respects. Commercially, for the good of the whole community; politically, for Imperial

interests; and militarily for the protection of, and to hold the country against, our neighbours at some future day; also for all purposes of convenience to the local government in connection with Vancouver's Island, at the same time as with the back country. It is a most important spot. It is positively marvelous how singularly it is formed for the site of a large town. It is not only convenient in every respect, but it is agreeable and striking in aspect. Viewed from the Gulf of Georgia across the meadow on entering the Frazer, the far distant giant mountains forming a dark background, the city would appear throned Queen-like and shining in the glory of the mid-day sun.

I have urged the matter (site of city) very earnestly on the Governor in a military point of view and he has promised to send my letter home. He admits all my facts, so does Judge Begbie, approves of my policy, and we have drawn up a proclamation in which it is stated that a town is to be laid out (at my site), which is to be the port of entry, and the Capital of British Columbia.[2]

Governor Douglas accepted Moody's selection for the new capital reluctantly, as he was likely disgraced about his own ill-conceived selection and expenditures at Derby. It is possible that he was still unsure of Moody's influence and how his own self-serving actions would be perceived by the Colonial Office, which was very suspicious of his ties to the Hudson's Bay Company. Moody had heard about the governor's Derby townsite at San Francisco on his way to the colony and had been "very much vexed." Upon arrival, he dismissed the desolate swampy site of Derby as lacking a harbour, being on the wrong side of the river and sitting too close to the American border to be defensible: "At any moment the Americans could and would have their grip on the very throat of British Columbia."[3]

Moody was delighted by victory when, on February 14, 1859, "Queenborough," named to honour Queen Victoria, was declared the capital of the new colony. Douglas, still peeved, delayed designating it as the port of entry until June 2. Property owners of Derby were informed that their lots could be surrendered and the money used to purchase lots in the new capital. Victoria land speculators such as Amor de Cosmos were outraged with the thought of more competition and higher lot prices. The whole affair marked the beginning of a very strained relationship between Moody and Douglas.

The citizens of Victoria, especially its prominent Derby investors, were jealous at the upstart city on the Fraser River they mockingly called the "Phantom City." Concerned about the threat to their economy, some prominent Victoria citizens loudly opposed the name of Queenborough as being too similar to their own. Douglas wrote to the Colonial Office in February, " ... we are desirous that Her Majesty should vouchsafe on further proof of her continued regard by signifying her will as to the name to be given to the future capital ... it will be received and esteemed as an especial mark of royal favor were Her Majesty to name the capital of British Columbia."[4]

In this view of Columbia Street at Lytton Square, the business section of the city has completed its first phase of development, transforming the former site of primeval forest. At left is the Hicks building, constructed in 1860–61, and beside it is Captain Millard's stone block, constructed at a cost of $40,000 in 1863. On the opposite side of the street is the famed Hyack Engine House with its tower constructed by the Hyack Engine Company in 1862. Hyack was a word meaning "fast" or "quick" and was used in the trade language of the coast known as Chinook Jargon, which was a mix of Aboriginal and European words.

CHARLES GENTILE PHOTOGRAPH, C. 1867.
IHP 0260

Access to New Westminster by ocean-going vessels was difficult because of the navigational hazards at the river's mouth. Early waterfront dock facilities were crude but fulfilled the needs of the few seagoing ships that made the trip up the river. In this view of the city's waterfront a sternwheeler has been pulled on shore for repairs. The ship at dock was the San Francisco-based Vickeray, *a barque that was the first to load cargo at the port of New Westminster.*

F.G. CLAUDET PHOTOGRAPH, SEPTEMBER 13, 1860. IHP 0077

Bulwer-Lytton agreed. He personally described the name Queenborough as not only prosaic—but vulgar! He wrote to the Queen on April 24, 1859, and provided three suggestions for her consideration: Regina, Augusta and New Westminster. Of the latter name, obviously of his own invention, he wrote that he was "… not aware that name has been given to any towns either in the United States or in your Majesty's Colonies and it being at once familiar to English association and transplanting to new shores. The name of the most ancient, most historical, and, so to speak, the most regal district of the metropolis, it may not be unworthy of consideration." Using the stationery from the royal house at Windsor, Queen Victoria responded four days later and, referring to herself in the third person wrote: "The Queen acknowledges Sir Edward Bulwer-Lytton's letter … She has chosen 'New Westminster' for the name of the Capital of British Columbia." [5]

When news finally reached the colony, the Queen's choice was not well received by some residents, who were less than royally impressed. Colonel Moody's private secretary, Robert Burnaby, wrote home, "We hear this town is to be renamed New Westminster which we all think is absurd. If they had called it C*anoe* Westminster we could better

understand." [6] Despite the mockery of some, the Queen's choice was widely approved and accepted. The selection of its name by Her Majesty would forever give the city the fame and claim of Royal favour such that its residents could justly boast their home to be the "Royal City."

New Westminster had started to emerge from the wilderness in the spring of 1859. Colonel Moody had made some progress on the survey of the town and had already decided on the location of the townsite and the military (sapper's) camp for the Columbia Detachment. The work of clearing the site was an enormous obstacle, of which he wrote to Governor Douglas:

> We are struggling here against very tiresome difficulties and delays arising from most atrocious weather. The rain is incessant and gusts with mists—snow half thawed is deep throughout the woods—the thickets are the closest and thorniest I ever came across. My clothes are becoming ragged! And the men's hands are torn in every direction. I am sending to Victoria for some stout strong common leather gloves for them if such can be procured. It will be repaid in saving time and money. I stand by and sometimes help a little, so I see with my own eyes what a loss of time it is giving a wince and rubbing your hand when a thorn as big and as strong as a shark's tooth tears across it.
>
> The woods are magnificent, superb beyond description but most vexatious to a surveyor and the first dwellers in a town. I declare without the least sentimentality, I grieve and mourn the ruthless destruction of these most glorious trees. What a grand old Park this whole hill would make! I am reserving a very beautiful glen and adjoining ravine for the People and Park. I have already named it 'Queen's Ravine' and trust you will approve. It divides the town well from the military Reserve ... [7]

In this very first panoramic view of the city, New Westminster's earliest buildings are dwarfed by the huge forest, with magnificent trees towering over 200 feet tall.

F.G. CLAUDET PHOTOGRAPH, C. 1861.
NWPL 294, 298

The trail between the Royal Engineers' camp and the town developed into a fine extension of Columbia Street that became a popular stroll for residents to enjoy the spectacular views of the river and mountains.

There was much to do, and a sense of urgency pervaded the work, with the Thames City sailing around Cape Horn carrying the largest contingent of the Columbia detachment—Captain Luard and 121 men, with 31 wives and 34 children. Upon their arrival on April 12, 1859, they stayed at the log barracks at Derby until the completion of the self-contained sapper's camp. On June 27, 1859, they were joined by another contingent headed by Sergeant Rylatt and 4 men, 6 women and 4 children who arrived with a ship loaded with supplies. The sapper's camp came alive with its small population full of energy and spirit. By the end of 1859, the camp was a self-contained village, with the engineers' barracks, a guardroom and cells, storehouses and a powder magazine completed. The following year, all of the engineers were out of their canvas tents into barracks, and in 1861 a fine "Government House" had been completed for Colonel Moody and his family overlooking the river.

A mile downriver the new site of the Capital City was literally carved out of the forest; Moody's ambitious plan for a garden city was on paper in the form of a finely crafted civic plat. This map drawing showed the designated legal lots, roads, squares, parks and future public works. It was finely printed and coloured brightly with watercolours. However, Moody's ambitious fantasy on paper would remain far from reality. It took three months for the available Royal Engineers, Royal Marines and civilians to fell some of the trees and partially survey the site. The design of the city was conceived by Colonel Moody to conform to and take advantage of its natural topography and to maximize the length of the usable riverfront for commerce. Initially, the city plat was laid out only to Royal Avenue at the crest of the city's fine hill. The grid pattern established for the streets assisted with the ease of surveying in the

Opposite page: *The original plat of the City of New Westminster as drawn by Royal Engineer Lance Corporal James Conroy and printed by sapper William Oldham,* 1861.

IHX 987.3468

forest, where it would have been difficult for even the most experienced surveyor to keep a straight line.

The main thoroughfare of Columbia Street was designed to be a market street, while the riverfront was envisioned as docks. Front Street would have to wait for years—for the construction of its quay and tons of fill—before it would emerge. The high land to the east, with its spectacular views, was drawn as the exclusive high-class residential district adjoining the Queen's Ravine. As the focal point for this district, a garden or park was ringed by the drive Albert Crescent, named after Queen Victoria's consort, and planned with flanking river terraces named after princes Arthur and Alfred. Lands at the western end of Columbia, in the swamp, were wisely set aside for more docklands and the Merchant Square. At the centre of the city plat was the block reserved for "gardens" where, according to the plat, the government offices would eventually be located, overlooking the river from a high terrace below Royal Avenue. Further down the hill was Victoria Gardens and the site chosen for a future cathedral of the Anglican church, located in the heart of the city, overlooking Lytton Square on the waterfront.

The auction sale of lots took place on June 1 and 2, 1859, and was a great success, with 310 of the available 318 lots sold, yielding over $89,000. The auctioneer of the day was surrounded by the population of Victoria, eager to speculate in the phantom city. Finally, new immigrants to the colony could find a place to call home, in the new capital. Initially, they found nothing more than a clearing in a forest surrounded by 200-foot trees.

The auctioneer stated that the money raised from the land sales would be applied to the opening up of the new city's roads. However, the money was not spent immediately; Colonel Moody and his small force of men were spread too thin trying to accomplish much and Douglas refused to approve the expenditure for private contracts. Then, in August 1859, the San Juan Islands boundary dispute broke out and Lieutenant

In this image, taken from the corner of Douglas (now Eighth) and Columbia Streets, the whitewashed Customs House built in 1859 by the Royal Engineers stands in stark contrast to the "packing crate"-like homes and commercial buildings. Note that the swamp at the west end of Columbia Street necessitated the road to be raised and paved with logs.

F.G. CLAUDET PHOTOGRAPH, C.1861. NWPL 271

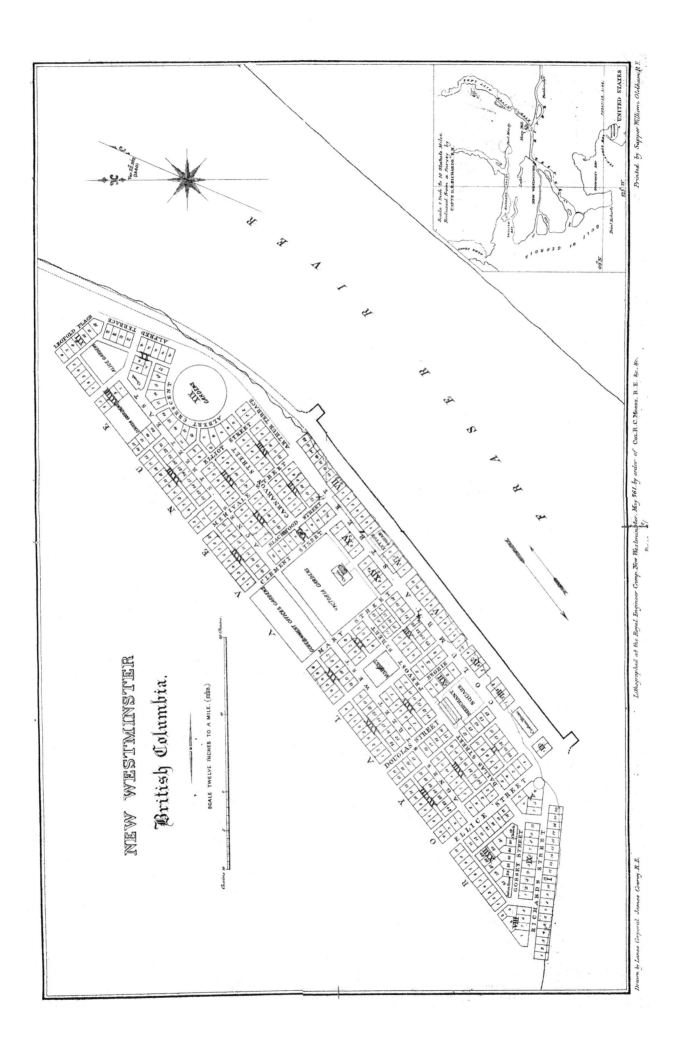

NEW WESTMINSTER
British Columbia.

SCALE TWELVE INCHES TO A MILE. (1:5280.)

FRASER RIVER

UNITED STATES

GULF OF GEORGIA

Scale 1 Inch, to 10 Statute Miles.
Reduced from a Survey by
CAPT.N G.H.RICHARDS R.N

Drawn by Lance Corporal James Conroy R.E.

Lithographed at the Royal Engineer Camp, New Westminster, May 1861, by order of Col. R. C. Moody, R. E. &c.

Printed by Sapper William Oldham R.E.

Lempriere headed out with 14 engineers and 48 marines to defend the interests of the crown. Although this left the corps even further behind in their work, the minor threat was enough to spook the Colonial Office into keeping the Royal Engineers in B.C. for a few more years.

Despite the slow progress, there were some signs that the city was becoming a reality thanks to the Royal Engineers. The stark white and rather plain government buildings were erected on the lots on Columbia Street. At the heart of the city, the Queen's church was given centre stage and the first Holy Trinity Church was built in 1860 surrounded by stumps and trees on a hillock between two ravines. Another sign of progress was the rough collection of early business blocks and homes built amid stumps—a landscape that led some critics to call this place the "Imperial Stumpfield."

Robert Burnaby described the atmosphere of the city:

> Being now in the midst of camp life and on the future site of a great city, I must try and convey to you some idea of our situation … Beyond the camp 2 or 3 wooden houses for officers etc. are building [*sic*], and on the space beyond, Col. Moody's house is to be. Further on, still following the river, there is a deep broad ravine, with a swift shallow stream running thro' it. Across this, after climbing up the other side, we came to the Marine camp, where 130 men and 6 officers are stationed … the trail to the town … has been chiefly cut by the Marines, it is a winding path thro' cedars and pine groves,

This two-part panorama of New Westminster was taken from Lytton Square. It shows the new Government Treasury and Assay Office, built in 1859–60 (Columbia Street and Mary [Sixth] Street), and the fine Gothic-styled Holy Trinity Church, dedicated in 1860, amid the stumps. The Government Bakery, opened by Philip Hick in 1859, was one of the city's first commercial enterprises. The two bridges were necessities for Columbia Street, as it crossed several deep ravines.

F.G. CLAUDET PHOTOGRAPH, C. 1861.
IHP 4304/ NWPL 324

On approach from the river, the site of New Westminster was indeed majestic even though its buildings were still dwarfed by the remaining forest.

SPEALIGHT NAVAL PHOTOGRAPH, C. 1868. IHP 7403

over logs across small streams for about a mile. All the way we go the axe resounds on every side, and high fires are burning up the heaps of brushwood.

So—there lies the town on the river bank, we wind down a slope to it, and behold about 2 dozen wooden shanties, with a sprinkling of tents and marquees, and here and there a canvas house, for all the world like Greenwich Fair. Here is the Hotel de Paris, where the guests sleep under the tables at night, where they cook you recherché dinners in the back yard. Next to it a small store, where you may buy hams, axes, beans, pork and flour, quicksilver, gum boots (India rubber), and all the mining luxuries. A little further the Pioneer Saloon, where they dispense liquors, cocktails and beer, and around which you see the miners in their red blue and white toggery, lounging and lazy, wondering over the prospects, and some disappointed ones coming back full of wrath and growling. A nigger barber has a shop about 6 ft. square, his chair made of a barrel covered with chintz, and his pole a branch cut from a neighbouring tree and some red and white paper twisted round it. Custom House and Treasury are rising a little lower down, both wooden but very pretty places, all around them lie the great trunks of timber like corpses on a battlefield, and you clamber over them continually ere you reach the Public Offices. Now there's a ringing of a fine toned bell tolling across the river, and you see a steamer, the Eliza Anderson, bringing goods and passengers from Victoria, few passengers, most of them bound for the upper country.[8]

Captain William Irving built the Onward *in Victoria in 1864. It was dubbed "the most luxurious steamboat to operate on the Fraser." It hauled passengers and freight between New Westminster and Yale and on one trip netted over $1,500. In this photograph the* Onward *has been commandeered for a Hyack Engine Company picnic and is docked near McLean's Ranch on the Pitt River.*

F.G. Claudet photograph, c. 1867.
IHP-IFP 0435

Many of the city's new residents were from Upper Canada, Nova Scotia and Newfoundland. They were well educated and ambitious and had gambled their life savings to come west and build fine dwellings and businesses, anticipating future greatness. Being accustomed to the responsible government of their old crown colonies, these new citizens were infuriated by the despotic acts and non-residence of Governor Douglas. Residents were frustrated by the lack of clearing and grading of new streets in the town. In their view, the colonial government had promised that these works would be financed with the proceeds of land sales realized at the first land auction. When a second sale of lots was arranged, disgruntled citizens shouted down the auctioneer, forcing the event to be rescheduled. A new tradition of civic politics had begun.

In January 1860, Douglas imposed a special duty on all wares and goods transported from New Westminster, while leaving Victoria as a free port. Boats all but passed the city in a direct line from Victoria to Hope, where miners would begin their trek to the goldfields. This blatant move to hamper the city's growth in favour of his home in Victoria made Royal City residents rally together. The rage of residents is reflected in the fiery editorials of John Robson, who had established *The British Columbian*, the city's premier newspaper, in 1861. Citizens demanded control of their destiny in the form of at least their own city council. Douglas relented, and on July 16, 1860, New Westminster was incorporated as a city with an elected municipal council, making it the oldest incorporated municipality west of Ontario.

This move on the part of the governor seemed calculated to appease the opposition to his rule in the city as well as to conveniently shift the tax burden of road construction directly onto citizens. The spite that Douglas had for the community was revealed in a letter in which he wrote that he "… had not yielded obedience to their sovereign will by cultivating the Canadian, in preference to the sound sterling English element in the Colony. A mass of other nonsense of the same kind has also appeared, in the columns of their organ [*The British Columbian*] to which I paid not the slightest attention, as I most thoroughly despise the whole of that contemptible clique." [9]

The citizens of the Royal City were soon forced to face the economic reality that the gold rush was not the "Eldorado" that had been initially hoped for. The Colonial Office realized the "mistake" that Bulwer-Lytton had made in sending the Royal Engineers, and in 1863 they were recalled. Only 22 officers and sappers, 8 wives and 17 children departed for home on November 11, 1863, when a crowd of citizens converged at the dock to say goodbye. The remaining sappers and their families chose to stay in the colony, and many became leading citizens. However, despite the optimism of the city's residents, more difficult decisions lay ahead.

In part, the efforts of reform-minded citizens of New Westminster were responsible for having Governor Douglas forced to resign his post

Governor Seymour left the colony to return home on an extended visit during which he married Miss Stapleton of Grey's Court, Oxford, in 1866. Governor and Lady Seymour were residents of the Royal City for a short time and their lavish spending on parties made many friends. In the end, the governor's inability to be decisive about the location of the capital proved a disaster for the city that had showed him such loyalty.

F. DALLY PHOTOGRAPH, C. 1867. NWPL 1170

Government House, built in 1861–62 for Colonel Moody, briefly housed the much-despised Governor Douglas in 1864. His replacement by Governor Seymour was greeted with a city-wide celebration. Seymour expended scarce funds on a large addition to the house, with an ornamental tower designed by a former Royal Engineer, architect J.C. White.

F.G. CLAUDET PHOTOGRAPH, C. 1865. IHP 0622

early and two new governors appointed. The arrival of the colony's own governor, Frederick Seymour, was met with a joyful celebration in the Royal City on April 20, 1864. A new legislature, consisting of 15 members, was also approved for the colony. As well, the Colonial Office agreed to convey some further concessions to the petitioners of New Westminster. Rather than all members of the legislature being officials appointed by the crown, one third of the members would be candidates that enjoyed the popular confidence of the citizens of the colony.

Governor Seymour discovered a city that was depressed and in financial uncertainty. It still had not been entirely freed from the forest, but to its credit, had a number of substantial buildings and established institutions that would have made any city proud. Captain Millard had built a stone and brick business block of substantial proportions designed by architects Wright and Sanders for the enormous sum of $40,000. The Hyack Engine Company occupied a fine engine house and the volunteer firemen wore smart red shirts, black pants and caps. Besides Holy Trinity Church there were now Methodist, St. Andrew's Presbyterian and St. Peter's Catholic churches. Some fine residences had been constructed in fine Gothic styles using imported California redwood for their construction. The city now even boasted the Royal Columbian Hospital, supported by public subscription and housed in an impressive building with a valuable bath provided by Colonel Moody.

The Governor was less than impressed with some of the utilitarian aspects of the public buildings. The public school was located in a small building near a bog and was dingy and infested with vermin. The governor soon ensured that it was relocated into a substantial building designed by former Royal Engineer and now private architect J.C. White in its own splendid square overlooking the city above Royal Avenue. The Government House was less than adequate for Seymour's needs but he commissioned White to design a large addition with a picturesque

In 1863 a group of about 70 to 80 residents of New Westminster, including some former members of the Royal Engineers, formed a defence force known as the New Westminster Volunteer Rifles. In 1866 this force was supported during the Fenian crisis by the creation of the Home Guards and the Seymour Artillery. In this photograph a group of 10 "crack shots" of the volunteers are seen standing after beating the navy (seated on lawn) in a prize match held on the cricket grounds. Governor Seymour is on horseback inspecting the scene. Left to right: A.T. Bushby (seated in chair), Captain Pritchard, Lieutenant A.N. Birch, Ensign R. Wolfenden, J.C. Brown, C. Good, I. Fisher, J.T. Scott, G. Williams, W.A. Franklin, R. Butler and Joseph Burr.

tower and lofty ballroom overlooking the Fraser. It was here that New Westminster celebrated in the style worthy of a capital city at the first of many balls and dances hosted by the extravagant governor. Sapperton was soon graced with a lovely English-styled country church, St. Mary's Anglican, another architectural delight designed by architect White in 1865. It was attended by the governor and other officials located in this hamlet that had first served as the Royal Engineers' camp.

Nothing, however, could fix the very grave financial situation. The colony was a drain on the British government and, despite the howls of protest, the two bitter rival colonies were united as a cost-saving measure on November 19, 1866. The only consolation to citizens of the mainland was that New Westminster remained the capital city. The legislature now would consist of 23 members, but the majority of votes remained those officials appointed by the crown, with only 9 popularly elected representatives from both the island and mainland.

The new legislative council, in which the majority of official appointments were Victoria residents, passed a resolution urging the relocation of the government seat and won by a vote of 13 to 8. Governor Seymour, who had the ability to overrule the decision, was increasingly ineffective. He was suffering physically from alcoholism, a condition that would take his life the following year. Seymour dithered, and instead of making a decision, placed a similar resolution before the legislative council, which passed by a vote of 14 to 5. A party of victorious Victorians celebrated at the Colonial Hotel, while a mob of revengeful citizens gathered outside, but in the end took no action.

Victoria was proclaimed capital city and, to add insult to New Westminster's injury, the proclamation took effect on the Queen's birthday, May 24, 1868. "Not only has Her Majesty's Government swindled the people of New Westminster, and that in the most bare-faced way, but her

Top: *Captain William and Elizabeth Irving constructed this lovely Gothic-styled villa in 1865. It was proclaimed by* The British Columbian *to be "… not only the handsomest, but the best and most home-like house of which British Columbia can yet boast." It remains remarkably intact today as a beautifully preserved historic house-museum owned and operated by the City of New Westminster at Royal Avenue and Merrivale Street.*

Photographer unknown, c. 1868. IHP-IFP 0369

Bottom: *The highly ornate house that William Clarkson built in the "Surburban Lands" at Pelham (Third) Avenue and Clement (Fourth) Street in 1864 was described as "one of the handsomest residences yet erected" by* The British Columbian. *Moved and renovated in 1911 to create two homes, it still stands today at 314 Pine Street and 313 Fourth Street.*

F.G. Claudet photograph, c. 1866. IHP 0350

Top: *New Westminster had a notorious number of saloons in its early days. "The Retreat" was built in Sapperton by Messrs. Howson and Hilliard in 1861 and served the Royal Engineers at the camp. It was conveniently and scandalously located adjacent to St. Mary's Anglican church.*

F.G. Claudet photograph, c. 1862. IHP 7776

Bottom: *Reverend Edward White and his parishioners constructed the first Methodist Church on Mary (Sixth) Street with their own labour. It opened for service in 1860.*

Photographer unknown, c. 1860. IHP 1008

Members of the first Parliament of B.C. pose for this historic occasion outside the legislative building, the former main barracks at the Royal Engineers' camp. Left to right: H. Holbrook, G.A. Walken, W.O. Hamley, C. Brew, H.M. Ball, A.N. Birch, C.W. Frenks, P. O'Reilly, W. Moberly, J.A.R. Homer, H.P.P. Crease.
CHARLES GENTILE PHOTOGRAPH, 21 JANUARY 1864. IHP 0203

This magnificent three-part panorama of New Westminster shows both the remarkable progress of the town and why it was once called the "Imperial Stumpfield." Photographer Francis G. Claudet was transported to this river sandbar by the Sto:lo boatsmen, who managed to paddle their canoe into every frame to provide perspective for the composition.

F.G. CLAUDET PHOTOGRAPH, C. 1866. NWPL 278, LEFT. IHP 0618, CENTRE. IHP 2914, RIGHT.

representatives, with refined cruelty, have selected the Queen's birthday, a day which has always been enthusiastically celebrated here, as that upon which to crown the perfidious act..." [10] A memorial was immediately sent to the Queen on behalf of the municipal council and the people—but to no avail. Nevertheless, Her Majesty's birthday was marked faithfully, despite the bitter disappointment.

New Westminster, founded with such enthusiasm and hope by its dedicated residents, was severely wounded by this loss. A state of economic panic and depression descended upon the town and its citizenry as, within weeks, the seat of government was dismantled and moved across the Strait. Even its long-time political champion, John Robson, made the move, conceding defeat. The population, estimated at 1,800 in 1862, dropped during that calamitous year of 1868 to less than 500. The golden future of prosperity once dreamed of by the Royal City's citizens appeared lost forever. ✖

The Gentleman Photographer Francis George Claudet, 1837–1906

New Westminster owes so much to Francis George Claudet, a true English gentleman and the first photographic artist to capture the spirit of our city. More than any written documents, these photographs offer a glimpse of the extremely rough conditions encountered when the city was carved out of the forest.

Born in London, England, in 1837, Francis George Claudet was the youngest son of an eminent pioneer of photography, Antoine Claudet. Antoine is famed for his improvements to Daguerre's invention to make photography commercially viable. Rather than follow in his father's footsteps, Francis was educated at London's University College and assisted his brother Frederic, a well-known assayer.

The colonial secretary approved the establishment of an assay office and mint to serve the new goldfields of British Columbia. Claudet was recommended by the master of the royal mint to oversee the operation to be based in the capital city. In preparation for his first assignment as an assayer he went on to take a mining and metallurgy course at Caroline College in Braunschweig, Germany, in 1858–59.

Arriving in New Westminster in 1860, Claudet described the town as "a perfect chaos" and settled in to accomplish his assay work. Claudet's camera, ordered in London and shipped overseas, finally arrived and he began to photograph the landscape around him so he could send images home to his family. He captured some of the most stunning scenes of the founding of the Royal City. These photographs were even prized in their day and a selection were sent off to the London International Exhibition of 1862, earning Claudet an honorable mention.

In 1872 the assay office was ordered closed and Claudet returned to London the following year. Because of Claudet's keen eye and superb technical skills, the Royal City is captured in these treasured photographs that serve as significant historic documents of our remarkable founding. •

Above: Portrait of F.G. Claudet. Photographer unknown, c. 1858. nwpl 1655

CHAPTER 2

1868–1887

Freshwater Terminus

Previous page: *In just a decade, the city had accomplished so much, transforming a forest into an important settlement, with such impressive buildings as Holy Trinity Church, seen in the centre of this riverfront panorama.*

New Westminster's first May Day celebration took place on the cricket grounds overlooking the river. The Hyacks pose in their handsome uniforms with their captain and his assistant holding speaking trumpets. The first May Queen, Miss Helen McColl, stands on the Hyack's ladder wagon, high above her "loyal subjects."

I n the wake of the loss of its status as capital, New Westminster entered a new era that began with a profound sense of loss and melancholy. This inspired civic leaders to lift spirits by celebrating the future of their city as embodied in their children. The Hyack Engine Company, which had always been a key social group, hastily organized a children's May Day celebration in 1870. The symbolic optimism of May Day, representing renewal and rebirth, was lost on no one. In her speech of 1871 the May Queen said:

> … this crown wreath'd as it is with bright, bright flowers, emblems of innocence and of purity, you will find that no act of mine has sullied or tarnished its brightness. For the present, for today at least, with your permission I will set aside that dignity which generally characterizes royalty, and join with you, in your efforts to make this day a day of happiness, a day of pleasure for all of us, let the troubles of the past, and the anxiety of the future, be forgotten amid the pleasures of today. Let us forget our sadness, and clap our hands with gladness, and shout a joyous welcome, to this our bright May Day.[1]

Community spirit was further celebrated every May in the traditional honouring of Queen Victoria's birthday on May 24. In fact, the city had never failed to honour this occasion. The first royal salutes by cannon or rifle fire were accomplished by the Royal Engineers and then carried on by the New Westminster Volunteer Rifles, a company formed by residents. When Governor Seymour received a salute on his arrival in 1864, he was surprised that it was "simply loud explosions of gunpowder placed between two anvils, one of which on each occasion was blown into the air." [2] In 1866 the Seymour Artillery Company was formed, and in October 1867 they received two old-fashioned 24-pounder howitzers on wheeled field carriages from the British Army. The first proud and proper royal salute using these imperial guns was carried out in May 1868.

However, the old guns used by the Seymour Artillery Company were often in a terrible, even dangerous state of repair. It was reported one year:

> Application had been made to the local authorities at Victoria for permission to use the cannon here in firing a salute in honour of Her Majesty's Birthday. And the answer was—no cannon, the salute will be fired in the capital. It is high time to give the Island of Vancouver a good wholesome dose of home rule. Everything is reserved for that barren island. Our citizens were indignant when they heard of the refusal to let them use their own guns in saluting Her Majesty, but Chief Bonson and a crowd of loyal citizens got possession of an anvil and with twenty-one rounds they waked the echoes far beyond the Fraser. In the Royal City it is a strange sight to see loyalty packing anvils to be used as heavy guns in celebrating Her Majesty's birthday. But Canadian loyalty is very strong. The refusal to permit our volunteer officers to use our own guns on this occasion was a most disreputable proceeding.[3]

Below, right: *Taking a close-up portrait of a crowd was a rare feat for pioneer photographers, as it required everyone to hold perfectly still for the camera to capture the image. For the May Day portrait of 1871, the young girls of the city sit with solemn faces for the camera; those who moved ruined their image with a blur. At the base of the maypole (top centre) the first May Queen, Helen McColl, sits beside newly crowned Nellie Irving, who is wearing her medal known as the "Order of the Gold Star," presented by the Hyack Engine Company.*

PHOTOGRAPHER UNKNOWN, 1871. IHP 0295

To this day, the Ancient and Honourable Hyack Anvil Battery, formed by loyal residents, continues its proud and unique salute to Queen Victoria. Only on May 24, 1901, following the death of the sovereign, did the battery remain silent, out of respect for Her Majesty. Both May Day and Queen Victoria's birthday, imbued with the pageantry of the past and optimism for the future, would continue to define the city's spirit and serve as an annual celebration of its proud heritage.

New Westminster's loyalty to the crown also extended to support the proposal to join British Columbia into Confederation with Canada in 1871. The idea was the subject of much debate and wide-spread dissention, until the terms of entry into the union included the promise of the construction of the transcontinental railway. New Westminster's residents and investors seized upon this fantastic dream to carry them through the hard times. The House of Commons in Ottawa accepted the terms of Confederation and the new Dominion of Canada that spanned the continent was approved by Queen Victoria on July 20, 1871.

The officers of the Seymour Artillery Company pose in their fine uniforms and regalia as they plan strategy to fight for the defence of New Westminster at their Albert Crescent battery.

PHOTOGRAPHER UNKNOWN, C. 1885. IHP 0626

The Seymour Artillery Company stands at attention with their "Crimean War" cannons at the Albert Crescent battery. The deplorable condition of these cannons led to orders from Victoria that they not be fired during the annual 21-gun salute on the Queen's birthday in 1886. Patriotic citizens organized the first firing of the salute using anvils in place of the cannons and the Hyack Anvil Battery was born. These cannons are now located in front of city hall on Royal Avenue.

PHOTOGRAPHER UNKNOWN, C. 1885. IHP 4500

The civic arch of welcome for the visit of the Governor General of Canada, Lord Dufferin, was being constructed across Columbia Street with banners on either side reading "Our Sea Farm-Natural Resources." The banners celebrated the Fraser River salmon industry, using its trademark boxes and barrels in pyramids. Note the addition of salmon and sturgeon hanging in nets, which likely added a smelly odour to the celebration.

PHOTOGRAPHER UNKNOWN, 1882. IHP 1902

The old Customs House at Columbia and Begbie streets was handsomely landscaped and decorated to welcome the Queen's representative, Lord Dufferin.

PHOTOGRAPHER UNKNOWN, 1882. IHP 0316

Economically, the city struggled to overcome the stranglehold that Victoria maintained as a free port. Everything imported into British Columbia that was not smuggled was routed through that hated city, including the subsidized mail steamers, putting mainland ports at a disadvantage. In spite of this situation, local resources began to be exploited and New Westminster reaped the rewards of being the first commercial centre on the mainland.

One of the most important construction projects was the Westminster & Yale Wagon Road. Completed in 1874, this road funnelled all Fraser Valley travellers and settlers to the city. Alexander Ewen established the first commercial cannery on the Fraser River in 1870 and by 1878 there were eight canneries that produced more than five million cans of salmon annually. The lumber industry that had started in the city in the 1860s was strengthened by the establishment of mills nearby at Burrard Inlet; these additional mills provided employment and attracted other supporting industries.

The terms of Confederation also earmarked federal funds to establish a penitentiary. New Westminster's convenient location on the mainland won the site selection over Victoria. Following this decision, the city

The once-proud government buildings and their grounds at Columbia and Mary (Sixth) streets look forlorn and shabby, the result of the city's depressed economy following the collapse of the gold rush. Left to right: "Jim Indian," V.R. Tait, Dr. Black, A.T. Bushby, W.J. Armstrong, Captain Ball, T. Morey, H.V. Edmonds, Jack Fannin, and F.G. Claudet. Note that Claudet likely had someone's assistance to take this photograph.

F.G. CLAUDET PHOTOGRAPHER, 1871. IHP 0619

also became the preferred location for the new provincial asylum. The site chosen for the two institutions comprised the former Royal Engineer's camp and the Queen's Ravine set aside as one of the city's pleasure grounds. Sadly, the completion of the penitentiary in 1877 and the asylum in 1878, although lauded as a tremendous economic benefit to the struggling city, would ultimately remove the romantic and idyllic Government House and cricket grounds from public use and enjoyment. Other investments, such as the construction of the beautiful St. Ann's Convent and its lady's college atop Albert Crescent in 1877, also signalled the beginning of the return of prosperity for the city.

Citizens remained anxious about the future of the city as the final location of the Canadian Pacific Railway (CPR) line was debated. Influential politicians and businessmen of Victoria were certain that they could secure the terminus through a northern route via Bute Inlet and an extravagant ocean crossing at Seymour Narrows. New Westminster residents, boiling at the notion that Victoria could swindle another victory, charged into the political battle claiming their "outer harbour" at Burrard Inlet as the superior choice. In 1878, after a hotly contested debate, the federal government finally announced that the railway would terminate at Port Moody. Royal City residents revelled in their victory and the justly deserved rejection of Vancouver Island. The city's old champion, John Robson, even returned from his exile in Victoria to resume his role as the editor of *The British Columbian* newspaper.

The first railway contract was awarded to Andrew Onderdonk, and in 1881 hundreds of workmen began to pass through New Westminster on their way to the work camps upriver. Among the new railway workers were Chinese labourers who were treated and housed poorly. During the influx, there was a near riot when about 900 Chinese men, who fought each other in two distinct factions, were penned up on the docks overnight like "cattle."

These new immigrants decided to invest in the city and make it their home by creating a colourful and distinct Chinatown at the eastern end of Front Street. The racism against the Chinese was obvious in reports printed in local newspapers, like this one:

> The smell of roast cabbage, cats and sin pollutes the air in that part of Front Street north of Melody's Saloon. Surely it is time for City Fathers to think of removing the Celestial iniquities to a place somewhere outside the city limits. If they will not or cannot do so, let them insist on having the laws of decency observed and compel the Celestial population to shut up the traps into which young men are enticed by Indian women and opium. The private history of the north end of Front Street is fit for publication in the lower regions, but no other place.[4]

This Sapperton wilderness was home to two institutions critical to the revival of the city's dismal economy prior to 1886. The provincial asylum built on the old cricket ground is surrounded by a forest of stumps. Across the "Queen's Ravine" can be seen the new penitentiary and the tower of the forlorn Government House.

Photographer unknown, c. 1885. IHP 1714-12

The federal government funded the construction of the new British Columbia Penitentiary as part of its agreement for B.C. to join Canada in 1871. This historic building still stands today, a landmark of Sapperton.

<small>Photographer unknown, c.1877. IHP 1714-2</small>

Many residents saw the Chinese as a curious and exotic addition to the city. In 1886, hundreds witnessed a grand display of fireworks put on by the local Chinese community and happily participated in their New Year celebration.

With all the construction activity, the city soon had hundreds of men looking for hotels and entertainment and the population increased to 1,800, according to the official census. It was said that the Royal City grew to become a "rip roaring town of 3,000 with 17 saloons open all night and seven days a week—a Waterloo for the miners and loggers from outside."[5] In response to all this activity, both throughout the region and in the town's "den's of iniquity," the province built a new gaol in 1885, located west of Douglas (Eighth) Street near Toronto Place. It could house over 90 prisoners.

The agricultural district of the Fraser Valley was developing extensively during this era. This resulted in the city becoming an important transportation and supply centre for farmers. The business community rallied to incorporate the Board of Trade in 1882–83. City council seized upon the new economy to construct a combined "Agricultural Hall and

Immigrant Shed" on Market Square in 1883. This facility served the important function of housing new immigrants upon their arrival until accommodation could be found. The hall also found a ready use in October 1883, when the mainland's first "Provincial Exhibition," featuring the agricultural and industrial wares produced in the region, was opened by Premier Smithe. In 1886 the old New Westminster District Agricultural Society, incorporated in 1867, was transformed into the Royal Agricultural and Industrial Society of British Columbia. The society's exhibitions served as important promotional events, lifting the spirits and pride of the city and district.

On November 7, 1885, excitement and anticipation greeted the arrival of the first train to Port Moody after the last spike ceremony. New Westminster's residents remained focussed on the goal of securing a "branch railway." Civic leaders took steps to invoke a railway charter invested in "The New Westminster and Port Moody Railway Company" formed by leading citizens. In order to raise the needed construction bonus, city council decided to request title of its numerous reserves and squares from the province and subdivide many of them to auction the lots.

The lands put up for auction included Victoria Gardens, St. Patrick's Square, Clinton Place Reserve, Merchant's Square, St. George's Square, and St. Andrew's Square. All of these parks and public areas had been

The construction of the boarding house known as the Farmers' Home on Church Street reflected the growth of the agricultural district of the Fraser Valley and the importance of New Westminster as a central hub for supplies and distribution.

PHOTOGRAPHER UNKNOWN, C.1885. IHP 4391

designed by Colonel Moody as part of the original plan for the garden city. Their sale would forever change its character and rob the city of an incredible legacy. The bylaw drew immediate denouncements from vocal citizens who felt that the sale of these public properties would not only destroy the beautiful design of the city but would devalue their private property. One property owner who owned land fronting on Merchant Square even took the case to the Supreme Court of B.C. in a failed bid to try and stop the auction. Despite this opposition to the bylaw, eligible voters passed it virtually unchanged by 96 to 26.

Many prominent businessmen of the city approved of the venture and many hedged their bets by investing in Port Moody, opening businesses and buying lots there. In 1886, CPR president William Cornelius Van Horne and the provincial government announced an agreement they had made to extend the railway line to a new terminus at Coal Harbour and English Bay. This deal would transform the sleepy lumber town of Granville into the city of Vancouver. The public was stunned by this decision, as personal investments gambled on the success of Port Moody were lost instantly. The agreement also included a clause designed to appease New Westminster with a plan to finance and construct a branch line to the transcontinental railway. A $75,000 cash bonus was to be paid to the CPR, with the cost being split by the province and the

Columbia Street on a hot summer afternoon in 1885 looks like the main street of a ghost town. This view is taken from Eighth Street looking east.

Photographer unknown, 1885. IHP 8005-02

Above: *The federal government finally recognized the growth of New Westminster's commercial district and built the Dominion building for the post office and customs office in 1884 to replace the old government building at the corner of Columbia and Mary (Sixth) streets.*

S.J. Thompson photograph, c. 1889. ihp 0170

Below: *This view of the intersection of Columbia and Eighth streets shows the small town on the cusp of the arrival of the CPR, which would transform New Westminster practically overnight into the "metropolis of the Fraser Valley."*

Photograper unknown, 1885. ihp 8005-01

city. However, the city also needed to secure the necessary right-of-way and depot grounds.

There was a hastily organized "riot" held by some livid Port Moody investors who knew that they had lost any chance of profit, or even of return, on their land. Many of the protesters felt the terms of the branch railway would be difficult to achieve and were designed for failure.

> Angry groups at every corner denounced [the district's Members of the Legislative Assembly, including John Cunningham, James Orr and John Robson, the provincial secretary ... the traitors who had betrayed the city ... four Indians came out of the alley; three of them carried aloft the life size figures of the three men suspended by ropes around the necks and fastened to poles; the fourth carried a frame ... with the inscription "Come witness the death of the traitors, who sold the city. So perish all traitors." The Indians marched down Columbia Street followed by the crowd. A number of persons carried empty coal oil cans and by taps and yells produced the most unearthly sounds. They visited Mr. Cunningham's private residence but he had warning and sought sanctuary in the Methodist Church. One of the boys shouted "the thief is at prayer" ... and on they rushed ... but the counsels of wisdom prevailed ... the horrid figures ... [were lit and] consumed to ashes, the crowd howling, the cans rattling and everyone willing to lend a hand or do something worse.[6]

Cooler business heads prevailed over this spectacle of a mock lynching and residents got down to business after several raucous meetings. The terms of the branch line financing were met on time by the city's issuance of debentures that were purchased by local investors. On November 27, 1886, the public auction of the city reserves and gardens took place at the

Below, top: *The new Colonial Hotel, built with brick, replaced the hotel lost to fire. It was designed by Victoria architect S.C. Burris in 1884.*

PHOTOGRAPHER UNKNOWN, C. 1886. NWPL 285

Below, bottom: *The grand Colonial Hotel was designed by architect James Kennedy for P. Arnaud in 1875. It was destroyed in a spectacular fire in 1883.*

PHOTOGRAPHER UNKNOWN, C. 1876. IHP 0173

Agricultural Hall and was a financial success. All of the funds needed to pay off the debentures for the branch railway had been realized.

The construction of the branch line was inaugurated on April 22, 1886, with an auspicious sod-turning ceremony held in Sapperton.

> The day was fine ... and every elevated place in the immediate neighbourhood was occupied by those who were most anxious to witness the interesting ceremony. The branches of the old trees groaned under a load of spectators, and some of the Chinese ventured to go aloft, among the leaves ... the artillery and rifles commanded by Captains Bole and Peele, preceeded by the College Band and followed by Chief Bonson and members of the St. Andrew's Society in tartans ... ... formed a hollow square round the spot chosen for the ceremony ... Mr. James Leamy, the contractor, advanced with a gaily decorated spade and presented it to Mrs. Dickinson [the Mayor's wife] and she with a little effort but in the most graceful manner, turned over the first sod. A solemn silence ensued; everyone expected to hear something—a speech, a song, or a sermon. And sure enough, they did hear something unusual. At the signal from Captain

Canada's first prime minister, Sir John A. Macdonald, visited the city and was greeted with a celebration organized at the old Government House, which was looking sad and neglected after a decade of remaining unused.

PHOTOGRAPHER UNKNOWN, AUGUST 18, 1886.
IHP 1714-8

Below: *Mayor Robert Dickinson (at left) presided over the sod-turning ceremony in Sapperton for the construction of the CPR branch line to the city. Contractor James Leamy is seen presenting the ceremonial shovel to Mrs. Robert Dickinson, who will do the honours on this historic occasion. The shovel survives to this day as a prized artifact of the New Westminster Museum.*

PHOTOGRAPHER UNKNOWN, APRIL 22, 1886.
IHP 8003-001

Bole the brass cannon thundered a salute. The ladies bounded like fawns; some of them cried "Oh," one or two turned pale but did not faint, and two Chinamen who had been nestling in the leaves of a sycamore tree tumbled off the branches like ripe pears ... [7]

By August 1886, it was reported that the "whistle of the locomotive has at last been heard in our midst; the construction train with all its boarding and lodging establishment reached Laidlaw's wharf yesterday morning. The long line of Chinamen occupied in grading, the whites laying the rails and the locomotive Kamloops with the train of section cars had a great attraction for our citizens and large numbers gathered to witness the novel scene." [8] The branch left the CPR mainline at "Westminster Junction" in what would become the future municipality of Coquitlam. The line entered the city far away from the river, but upon crossing the Brunette River, followed the riverfront downtown parallel to Front Street. The station site was at the western end of Columbia at Douglas (Eighth) Street, where soon a wooden station would rise adjacent to some modest railway sheds.

Canada's first prime minister, Sir John A. Macdonald, and Lady Macdonald embarked on an official tour over the completed sections of the Canadian Pacific Railway through Western Canada. They even took to riding on the train's cow-catcher through the mountains to enjoy a thrilling view of the grand scenery. New Westminster was selected as the location of a luncheon and celebration for the prime minister held at the old Government House on August 18, 1886.

Right: *This rare photograph captures CPR engine #374 on the day of its ceremonial arrival in the Royal City over the branch line. It also served as the ceremonial train for Vancouver's connection six months later and is preserved to this day in that city at the Roundhouse Community Centre.*

PHOTOGRAPHER UNKNOWN, NOVEMBER 1, 1886. NWPL 2278

Below: *The neat station and freight sheds at the foot of Eighth Street on the waterfront were the tangible evidence that the Royal City's long-held dream of being connected to the transcontinental railway had been fulfilled.*

NOTMAN PHOTOGRAPH, 1887. NWPL 906

1776—NEW WESTMINSTER, B.C.

WM. NOTMAN & SON, MONTREAL

The completion of the railway connection immediately spurred investors to purchase land in the city and many entrepreneurs began to transform the town with new industry, business and residences. The boastful *British Columbian* stated:

> The building improvements of New Westminster had been more marked this year than any in its history. A new life having been infused into the old capital ... and its citizens have been encouraged to look forward to a bright future and have gone into improvements of an extensive and purely metropolitan character. The effort has not only been to make buildings of fine dimensions and substantial qualities, but of beautiful proportions as well. In this the churches have taken the lead, and have shown an example ... The dwellings erected during 1886 are also in advance of previous years as to the size and beauty of design, and will no doubt lead to a most desirable rivalry and the adoption of the most modern patterns ... the gasworks ... together with the railway has wrought a change upon the complexion of affairs which is noticeable on every hand.[9]

The total construction value of $250,000 in 1886 was proclaimed as a splendid record. The New Westminster Gas Company was responsible for the largest construction works at its west end site at a cost of $65,000 to supply gas for interior and street lighting in 1886. The Catholic community in the Royal City showed its confidence with enthusiasm and a major building program. St. Peter's Church was completed in 1886 at a cost of $10,000, which added a magnificent 150-foot landmark spire

Sir John A. Macdonald, wearing a top hat, enjoyed a tour of the city given by James D. Fitzsimmons, Chief Keeper of the Dominion Penitentiary. The wagon is at the corner of Columbia and and Mary (Sixth) streets.

Photographer unknown, August 1886.
IHP 8003-002

Right: *The unusual* K de K *was the first scheduled ferry to operate on the river linking New Westminster to Surrey and the wagon road to the Fraser Valley in 1884.*

PHOTOGRAPHER UNKNOWN, C. 1889. IHP 0146

Below: *The* William Irving, *built by Captain John Irving in 1880 at Moodyville on Burrard Inlet, was one of the handsomest of the new Fraser River sternwheelers serving the new passenger and freight traffic that came with the railway construction boom.*

PHOTOGRAPHER UNKNOWN, C. 1886. IHP 0314

Above: *St. Mary's Hospital opened in a splendid new building in 1886 at the corner of Agnes and Merrivale streets as a charitable hospital operated by the Sisters of Providence, who also took on paying customers to keep up with the bills.*

<small>PHOTOGRAPHER UNKNOWN, 1886. IHP 647</small>

to the city's skyline of squat roofs. St. Mary's Hospital, a much needed charitable medical facility undertaken by the Sisters of Providence, was also a substantial $10,000 improvement. The Baptist congregation, not to be outdone, built another landmark of which the city could boast, the very pretty brick Olivet Church on Agnes Street.

On November 1, 1886, one year after the first train had arrived in Port Moody and seven months before Vancouver would greet its first train, the Royal City greeted the arrival of the first passenger train from the east with another ceremony. New Westminster had achieved a tremendous victory in securing its future and it proclaimed itself as the "Freshwater Terminus" of the greatest railway in the world. ✿

Below: *The rickety old wooden tower of Holy Trinity was demolished and a new cornerstone dedicated by Bishop Sillitoe, with the intention of erecting a new stone tower to house the bells donated by Lady Burdett Coutts. This tower was not completed until 1899. On the hill behind the church can be seen the old 1865 schoolhouse with cupola and the new school erected on Royal Avenue and Mary (Sixth) streets.*

<small>PHOTOGRAPHER UNKNOWN, APRIL 10, 1886. IHP 0647</small>

<small>48 ROYAL CITY</small>

Right: *Lawyer Gordon E. Corbould built this fine villa in 1886 on Pelham (Third) Street near Royal Avenue at a cost of $6,000. It was a grand and Gothic addition to the growing district of fine homes near Queen's Park. In this view the Corbould children, Gordie and Alma, are on the steps and Lillie is seated on the grass.*

THOMPSON AND BOVILL PHOTOGRAPH, 1888. IHP 0902-40

Below: *An impressive addition to the city was "Gadshill," the fine home of Bank of B.C. manager Issac B. Fisher, situated at Blackwood and Carnarvon streets. Built circa 1882, it was a mark of the new-found confidence of influential investors in the future of the city. In the background is the old 1863 St. Andrew's Presbyterian church, which still stands as the city's oldest building.*

PHOTOGRAPHER UNKNOWN, C. 1886. IHP 0053

Above: *The Hyack Engine Company #1 proudly poses outside the Hyack Hall on Columbia Street along with its pumper wagon and the May Queen and suite in a carriage.*

PHOTOGRAPHER UNKNOWN, C. 1886.
IHP 0086

Right: *Inside the customs office of the Dominion building, government employees H.R. Dunn (statistician), A.R. Peele (clerk), Peter Grant (chief clerk) and James McMartin (clerk) enjoy the regal surroundings that finally gave New Westminster something to boast about.*

PHOTOGRAPHER UNKNOWN, C. 1889.
IHP 0108

Judkins Floating Sunbeam Gallery   DAVID R. JUDKINS, 1836–1909

David Roby Judkins was one of the most enterprising of New Westminster's early photographers. Many portrait photographers were faced with the trials of travelling to small communities to make a living. It must have been a struggle to lug heavy, fragile equipment and locate a rented space to convert into a temporary studio in every town. Judkins, based in Seattle from 1880–1884, conceived the rather ingenious and novel idea of building a studio on a barge. He would then contract with various steamboat operators to have it towed up and down the coast to various commercial centres. His gallery was dubbed "Judkins' Floating Sunbeam Gallery" and certainly caused a bit of a stir in every community that was visited.

Judkins and his barge were towed up the muddy Fraser River in June 1882 to be docked in New Westminster. Local newspapers eager for a story and advertising, commented on the unique studio and urged readers to avail themselves of the opportunity of getting a good quality photograph from this artist before he and his studio sailed away to the next community. The newspaper copy served as great advertising for Judkins, who appeared to have made the business a success. His stay in New Westminster only lasted for a few months; in September 1882 Captain Grant piloted the steamer Ada to tow the barge to Nanaimo and new patrons.

According to historian David Mattison, Judkins later left his floating gallery to operate the Pullman Photographic Gallery in Skagway, Alaska, in 1899. He relocated to San Francisco from 1903 to 1906 and died in Santa Maria, California, in 1909. ●

Above: Judkins adopted the use of a unique printed card for the communities he visited in order to mount his portraits. IHP 1954-62v

Judkins' portraits of New Westminster clients are extremely rare. **Far left:** New Westminster pioneer John C. Brown put on his impressive uniform and medal of the Seymour Artillery Company to get his photograph taken in the floating studio. Note the beautiful painted backdrop, silk curtains, plush furnishings and carpet.

D.R. JUDKINS PHOTOGRAPH, 1882. IHP 1954-62

Left: A very regal G.E. Corbould wears the traditional wig and robes indicating his status as a lawyer.

D.R. JUDKINS PHOTOGRAPH, 1882. IHP 0902-22

CHAPTER 3

Metropolis 1887–1898

Previous page: *A romantic view taken from Brownsville in Surrey shows how beautiful and idyllic the river setting of the Royal City was during its late Victorian period. This photograph also demonstrates the artistic skill of Thompson, who composed the scene with a seated figure posed to reflect in the small pool in the foreground.*

S.J. THOMPSON PHOTOGRAPH, C. 1897. IHP 0621

*T*he arrival of the Canadian Pacific Railway was a defining event in the history of New Westminster. It changed the almost-forgotten, old-fashioned colonial town into a potential metropolis in the eyes of its citizens and investors. The change was so overwhelming that one local reporter used all his allegorical might to explain the city's new appearance:

> … with the sweep of Time's magic sceptre, one revolution in the kaleidoscope of circumstance, and, lo, our fair city has changed from a rustic forest maiden, standing on her border of the native wood, finger on lip, surveying all the world before her and wondering, wondering much if she might safely venture forth and make one struggle—from this simple artless, timorous maid Westminster has blossomed forth into a queen of dignity, beauty and stately form. She has dropped the sweet freshness of the young days, it is true, but she has acquired what is greater, better, a well defined position among her sister cities, unlimited credit and future prospects that are filled with golden promise. The change has been marvellous, immense … Since the first faint glimmer of the New Year broke over the mountains … his majesty the Sun, has witnessed with us the birth and growth of many a stately edifice, solid and strong and graced with all the charms and fancy the architect could give.[1]

With New Westminster and its upstart "twin" or "sister" city, Vancouver, the people of the Lower Mainland could now mount a significant challenge to rival the economic and political strength long held by Victoria. Changes to the character of the Royal City were immediate and striking. The sounds of the hammer and trowel could be heard all over as the building boom transformed streetscapes practically overnight. George William Grant, an architect from Nova Scotia, came west to seek work in Vancouver in 1885. He relocated to the Royal City because of its tremendous growth and opportunity, and became the city's leading architect, substantially determining the city's visual character. The old wooden buildings of Columbia Street, with their quaint, old-fashioned verandahs and balconies, were almost entirely demolished. They were replaced with over 30 handsome brick and stone commercial blocks, many among the most substantial in the province.

Over $3 million was spent on construction of new commercial, institutional and residential buildings between 1887 and 1892. The total value of land assessments, which stood at a paltry $862,511 in 1888, soared to $7,572,440 by 1893. The city's population, estimated at 3,000 in 1888, grew to 7,432 in the official municipal census of 1892. This was the highest percentage of urban growth increase shown by any city in Canada, other than Vancouver. The Royal City's status as the second largest city in the province was quickly overtaken by the "Terminal City," but this fact did not seem to dampen the enthusiasm of citizens.

The city's newfound prosperity warranted the expansion of its boundaries in 1888–89 to include all of the suburban blocks laid out by the Royal Engineers. The city now included historic Sapperton and, with the inauguration of a new charter on January 1, 1889, the former military reserve located on the tip of Lulu Island, which would soon be called Queensborough. This expansion also substantially increased the taxation revenues that could be used to develop the city. A wagon bridge was constructed to the new territory of Queensborough, where over 600 acres of land, reclaimed through new dikes built by the city, were sold to pay for the works.

The hill overlooking downtown was crowded with homes and the city's churches, forming a unique urban landscape. The photographer is atop the James Cunningham home on Agnes Street, looking east to its intersection with McKenzie Street.

Below: *In a rare interior view of the electric power plant, the massive generators that produced electricity can be seen, with the large belts that supplied the turning power from the steam engines.*

Below, right: *New Westminster was extremely proud of her modern civic-owned and -operated utilities. This building, known as the "Electric Light Station," housed the steam-powered electric power plant designed by architect G.W. Grant and built in 1891 at the foot of Tenth Street. Note the wooden chute on stilts behind the plant; it brought sawdust from the nearby Royal City Mills to fuel the steam engines.*

In 1889, a "progressive" council was elected that took on the challenge of creating the urban infrastructure appropriate for a modern city. The old Royal Columbian Hospital was relocated from its unhealthy site in the midst of the city to a new modern building that looked like a country villa in the wilds of Sapperton. An ambitious waterworks system was established, with a steel supply pipe that connected the city to Coquitlam Lake over 12 miles away. The city even established its own electric power plant and turned on the first electric street lights in 1891; this made the recently installed gas lamps seem ridiculously outdated and put the nearly new gasworks at a serious financial disadvantage.

Over 33 miles of streets were graded and sidewalks installed. The city's new grid pattern of opened streets required systematic house numbering. The original street names were replaced with a rational system of numbered streets and avenues patterned after large eastern cities. Lost in the change were many of the wonderfully romantic original colonial names. Mary Street, named in honour of Mary Moody, the wife of the Colonel, became Sixth Street. Park Lane became First Street. However, civic patriotism and ties to England ensured that citizens refused to part with the names of Royal Avenue and Queens Avenue in lieu of First and Second Avenues.

Council also spent a lavish $50,000 on improvements to the city's public parks, which radically enhanced opinions of the beauty of the place. Finally, the plan devised so many year ago by Colonel Moody for a garden city became a reality. Albert Crescent was printed on the original city plat as a drive surrounding a circular Prospect Park, but had existed only as a sea of stumps beside the old cannon battery. The park was cleared and regraded and an elaborate terraced garden was created below the beautiful edifice of St. Ann's school and convent. Here an artistic little bandstand was erected for the Artillery Band to play "sweet music" in the summertime. In both Moody Square and Queen's Park, adjacent to the growing residential districts, burned stumps and brush were cleared away to create public recreation fields for sport.

It was at Queen's Park that outstanding public gardens designed by landscape gardener Peter Latham took shape. Hundreds of trees and shrubs, including beeches and horse chestnut trees imported from France, were planted with a view to creating a legacy for generations. Queen's Park was crowned with the province's finest exhibition building, a spectacular tribute to the Queen Anne Revival style. It was designed by G.W. Grant and showcased the monumental versatility of British Columbia lumber. The building replaced the old 1883 structure

In this view of Columbia Street, the photographer has set up his camera looking east in front of the new Masonic and Oddfellows blocks at Lorne Street, built in 1892. The end of the Victorian building boom is evident in this view, and it demonstrates how truly magnificent the street became in just one decade following the arrival of the railway.

S.J. Thompson photograph, c. 1895. IHP 1679

This vantage point, atop the James Cunningham home on Agnes Street near the corner of Eighth Street, provided the photographer with a splendid view of the river and the prosperous plant of the Royal City Planing Mills located on the waterfront at the west end of the city. The undeveloped forest and swamps of Queensborough seen in the distance have just been incorporated into the city limits.

THOMPSON AND BOVILL PHOTOGRAPH, 1888. IHP 1118

The Royal Agricultural and Industrial Exhibition week was started with a parade on Columbia Street. In this photograph the parade is in the midst of being organized, and some members of the Hyack Engine Company look decidedly bored and impatient in their elegant uniforms. Behind them stands the handsome new Hamley Block with its fantastic third-storey conservatory, which served as the sunlit Thompson's Photo Studio. In the street at the corner of Sixth are building materials for the Douglas-Elliot Block, which is under construction.

S.J. THOMPSON PHOTOGRAPH, 1891. IHP 7367

in Market Square. It could house 5,000 visitors and was built to overlook and provide a viewing gallery for the race track surrounding the new athletic fields. This landmark structure became the new home of the Royal Agricultural and Industrial Society's annual Provincial Exhibition.

The business community kept up with the city's efforts by establishing public conveniences for the metropolis on the Fraser. A charter for the Westminster and Vancouver Tramway Company was established to link the twin cities and a new electric railway line opened between Vancouver and New Westminster in 1891. This spawned the creation of the Municipality of Burnaby, which reigned in any potential future ambitions of the Royal City to expand northwards. Within the city limits the same company had the previous year inaugurated the Westminster Street Railway Company, which ran on the rail line with smaller streetcars to connect the city's downtown with its growing residential suburbs and the new attractions at Queen's Park.

Right: *The exhibition buildings at Queen's Park, seen here during the great fall "carnival" held in 1891, immediately provided the city with a glorious architectural landmark that made it clear the Royal City was capital of the Fraser Valley.*

S.J. Thompson photograph, 1891. NWPL 1976

Below: *The celebratory exhibition parade is finally underway in this photograph taken at the corner of McKenzie Street looking east up Columbia. The hotel bars and restaurants have emptied of their patrons, who fill the street to cheer on the parade of wagons headed for Queen's Park.*

S.J. Thompson photograph, 1891. IHP 7368-034

The growth in the city's industrial and manufacturing sectors was phenomenal and created an ever-increasing need for residences to house all the new immigrants. It was a point of civic pride that, according to an 1892 estimate, only about 15 percent of the homes built in the city were constructed for rental accommodation, with the rest built out of the earnings of homeowners or with money borrowed by local building loan societies on easy terms. Wealthy merchants and businessmen built some spectacular Queen Anne Revival-styled mansions, the favoured location being near Queen's Park, now referred to by some as "Nabob Hill." Others built less costly houses and cottages here, while the not-so-wealthy found lots nearby in the "West End," with spectacular views overlooking the Fraser delta.

The construction activity of the era sparked the establishment of secondary manufacturing in the lumber trade; all the "charms and fancies" of the Victorian era could now be applied to even the most humble cottage. The Royal City Planing Mills Company tripled its production capacity and became the largest manufacturer and employer in the city, with over 500 men on staff. Much of its production of both lumber and secondary products found ready markets across North America and overseas. The Brunette Sawmill in Sapperton and the huge McLaren-Ross Mill outside the city limits added to the ever-increasing industrial output of the region. Also of importance was the New Westminster brickyard, which, in 1892 alone, turned out over two million bricks.

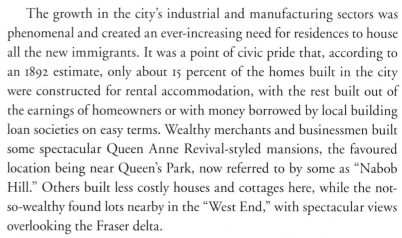

Below, top: *Taking down a monster tree in the woods surrounding New Westminster was no easy task. It required great physical strength and stamina and the ability to balance on a precarious springboard.*

Photographer unknown, c. 1889. ihp 0123

Below, bottom: *The waterfront in Sapperton became an industrial hub out of which grew this new suburb to house the workers and their families. The Brunette Sawmill, the largest of the local firms, and the Automatic Can Company, seen a quarter-mile upriver, were the first to locate here.*

P.L. Okamura photograph, c. 1894. ihp 0128

Top, left: *A testament to the riches of the salmon-canning industry was the home of canner Alexander Ewen, located at the corner of Begbie and Carnarvon streets. Its beautiful Queen Anne style was a $10,000 renovation to an old house, carried out by architect G.W. Grant in 1890.*

PHOTOGRAPHER UNKNOWN, C. 1894. NWPL 2726

Top, right: *"Blossom Grove," designed by architect G.W. Grant, was built for $25,000 by Henry Valentine Edmonds for his wife Mary in 1890 at Queens Avenue and First Street. It later became home to Columbian College until it closed; tragically, the house was demolished by the city in 1939.*

PHOTOGRAPHER UNKNOWN, C. 1896. NWPL 522

Bottom, right: *The manicured and terraced lawn-tennis courts of Dr. Fagan's residence at Carnarvon and Fourth streets were popular for summer parties that included both men and ladies of the New Westminster Tennis Club. The church is the Catholic Indian mission church known as St. Charles, built in 1884.*

S.J. THOMPSON PHOTOGRAPH, C. 1890. IHP 0760-02

In 1891, the city even acquired another railway connection to the United States. The New Westminster Southern Railway (Great Northern Railway) connected Fairhaven to "South Westminster," on the opposite side of the river. City council had negotiated with the province to place this portion of the Municipality of Surrey within its charter boundaries to ensure that its expenditure on public docks for the civic funded steam ferry *Surrey* here would be legal. Discussion towards building a bridge to link the city with the south side of the Fraser Valley and the United States now began amongst businessmen and politicians.

The old pioneer families and new residents of New Westminster responded to this remarkable era of progress with a tremendously optimistic civic spirit. Every conceivable religious and fraternal organization and society was formed, proving that the city was in every respect respectable. There were 18 churches, an astounding number for such a small city. A group of ladies even formed a branch of the Women's Christian Temperance Union and tried to reduce the number of drinking establishments, which shamefully now outnumbered the houses of God.

The New Westminster Band poses casually in a park, resplendent in smart uniforms.
TRUEMAN & CAPLE PHOTOGRAPH, C. 1892. IHP 0015

Below: *This romantic, beautifully composed image is an eastward view up the river and across Albert Crescent and the newly graded and terraced Prospect Park. The bandstand was built so the city band could play "sweet music" in the summertime.*

S.J. THOMPSON PHOTOGRAPH, 1891. IHP 0312

A strong sign of New Westminster's big-city status was its vice districts. At the eastern end of Front Street was the old Chinatown where Kwong On Wo and Company, the largest and most respected local Chinese importer, processed rice and opium for sale. Chinatown had rapidly expanded from its original location and began to occupy the lots west of Eighth Street in the district known as "the swamp." Here, the celebration of Chinese New Year attracted hundreds of "celestial" visitors from the district and filled the gambling houses to capacity. The city's prostitutes had their homes here too, and were referred to affectionately by the local press as "Swamp Angels." The ladies of the "dead-line" were notorious for the shame they brought to the city. Notable incidents of crime were all reported in the local newspapers with a fine mix of editorial outrage and salacious detail.

Despite the depravities of the swamp, the city progressed culturally at an admirable pace. Herring's Opera House could seat 800; in 1887, it was opened with a grand "Governor's Ball" presided over by British Columbia's Lieutenant-Governor Nelson. In a remarkable gesture towards the educational wealth of the community, the city even funded the construction of a $25,000 three-storey public library block in 1891; declared the largest and finest library west of Ontario, the building boasted opulent meeting rooms for the Board of Trade and the Mechanics' Institute. The educational needs of the community benefitted from the boom with a landmark brick Central School and new

Right: *In this photograph, trams of the Westminster and Vancouver Tramway Company and the little streetcars of the Westminster Street Railway Company meet to drop off passengers at Queen's Park, likely during the exhibition of 1892.*

S.J. THOMPSON PHOTOGRAPH, C. 1892. IHP 7949

Below: *The veranda of the Colonial Hotel was the perfect vantage point to view the band and cadets leading a parade for the May Queen. The Bank of B.C. Block at Columbia and Sixth seems small in comparison to the stately Douglas-Elliot Block.*

S.J. THOMPSON PHOTOGRAPH, 1896. IHP 4110

Westside and Sapperton schoolhouses designed to house the hundreds of new students. New Westminster even boasted the Columbian Methodist College, incorporated by the B.C. legislature in 1893 as the first institution of higher learning in the province.

The first indication that the good times were over came in 1892, when *The British Columbian* noted that lumber production had slipped. The world economy was severely affected by a drop in gold production, which supported the western world's currencies. The economy faltered and a full-scale bank panic ensued. The boom that had transformed New Westminster suddenly collapsed. Nearly overnight, a widespread economic depression ensued. *The British Columbian* reported that "Westminster escaped the larger disasters experienced elsewhere, and, though business has been slow, money tight and failures more numerous than usual, things on the whole might have been much worse." [2]

Despite this editorial writer's optimism, the local economy did get considerably worse. Unemployment was rampant, and in response, council hastily approved the hiring of 10 married men in each ward of the city

New Westminster was especially proud of those industrial concerns that indicated its progress beyond the usual resource industries. In this unusual interior view of the Vulcan Iron Works plant, workers have been carefully posed with their machines and tools, while the "captains of industry" form a party of inspection on the shop floor.

S.J. Thompson photograph, c. 1891. IHP 0176

Above: *A close-up view of a typical two-man fishing boat laying its nets with wooden floats on the muddy river alongside the Front Street wharfs. Lying in the boat is a sail rolled up on its mast.*

J.L. BROWNE PHOTOGRAPH, C. 1889. IHP 0096

Above, right: *It's a miracle that any salmon could get past the hundreds of boats and nets that comprised the "Fishing Fleet" at the mouth of the Fraser River.*

S.J. THOMPSON PHOTOGRAPH, C. 1891. IHP 0359

Right: *This scene of a fish-loaded cannery wharf epitomizes the damaging notion of the unlimited bounty and wealth of the Fraser River. Sto:lo workers, such as the woman and men posed here, were exploited as cheap labour by the canneries.*

S.J. THOMPSON PHOTOGRAPH, C. 1889. IHP 0360

Below, top: *This northeast view of the city was taken from the Powell Block overlooking the corner of Columbia and Church streets. It reveals many early businesses and architectural landmarks such as the Farmer's Home boarding house. Adjacent to this building is the Bovill Photo Studio with its rooftop skylights. Water vapour appears to be rising from the steam-driven Wintemute's Furniture Factory, located in the ravine. The new Anglican Bishop's Palace is being constructed on the hillside.*

PHOTOGRAPHER UNKNOWN, 1890. IHP 0070

Below, bottom: *The New Westminster City Market, built with taxpayer funds, was an immediate success with consumers and a huge asset to the economy, as it brought farmers from throughout the Fraser Valley to trade.*

P.L. OKAMURA PHOTOGRAPH, C. 1897. IHP 0098

for street improvements, at 20 cents an hour. To make matters worse, in May 1894 the Fraser Valley was hit by one of its worst floods ever. The Fraser River spilled over its banks and flood water tore through fields, leaving crops and cattle under water and farmers financially devastated. The city was not spared, as the waters flooded the lower areas and broke through the Lulu Island dikes in Queensborough. Also that year, fire destroyed the Royal City Mills, resulting in a claimed $55,000 loss. The Brunette Lumber Company too was hit by a huge fire in 1895, which threw many men out of work and resulted in a $78,000 loss—a severe blow to the economy of the city.

Recovery from this slump did not begin until the Klondike gold rush in 1897. The economy revived as manufacturers and suppliers in the city began to reap the benefits of providing supplies to the north. A further boost to the local economy came from those Klondike travellers from the United States who passed through the city via the Great Northern Railway, transferring to boats on their way to Dawson.

Along with the gold rush, the construction of some substantial landmark buildings built in 1896–97 also served to lift spirits. A new city market building, constructed on the waterfront at Lytton Square, proved to be a boon to both Fraser Valley farmers and the city. The old drill shed was deemed totally inadequate for the military company now known as the B.C. Battalion of Garrison Artillery–Company No. 4, and a new wooden armory was built at a cost of $7,000 at Queens Avenue and Sixth Street. Nels Nelson proved that beer survived every recession and built the Westminster Brewery in Sapperton.

The British Columbian could finally boast with confidence to its readers, after the close of 1897, that "we have weathered the blast … of depression and are now entering upon a new era of prosperity."[3] ✿

A Photographic Master STEPHEN JOSEPH THOMPSON, 1864–1929

Without question the pre-eminent photographer of New Westminster during the late Victorian period was Stephen Joseph Thompson. Born in Bailieboro, Ontario, Thompson was a talented artist of watercolour and pencil. Like so many other artists of his era he made the decision to learn photography to further his career opportunities and received training in his art in the refined centres of Montreal, Toronto and New York City. He travelled to British Columbia in 1886 and immediately saw the opportunity to establish himself in the Royal City, which was suffering from the lack of a large professional portrait studio.

With the headline "Our New Art Gallery," The British Columbian *ran in its edition of October 28, 1886:*

"The old photograph parlours on Columbia Street, opposite the Colonial Hotel, have been thoroughly renovated, and present now a very attractive and business-like appearance. The proprietors are Messrs. Thompson and Bovill. Mr. Thompson is a young gentleman who has recently arrived from the east, where he was the proprietor of a large gallery. He comes with the highest recommendations as to character and as an artist, both from the press and private parties, and will we believe be found a good citizen. The firm have imported new instruments, backgrounds, and all the accessories necessary to make first class work. They are prepared to give anyone a perfect facsimile of himself or herself, from miniature up to life size, and to do so at eastern prices, a fact worthy of consideration. We have no

hesitation in pronouncing samples of their work which we have seen equal if not superior to anything produced in the province, and we bespeak for them plenty of business."

The initial press was warranted, as Thompson was soon acknowledged as "one of the most skillful and best-known photographers on the coast." By 1888 he had dissolved the partnership with Bovill to operate successfully on his own and establish a marvelous new studio in the beautifully appointed Hamley Block on Columbia Street. A third-floor conservatory provided a landmark business icon for his retail trade and enabled him to conduct his business maximizing the available sunshine. Here he sold beautiful views of B.C. mountain scenery and city views for souvenirs. His work was regularly shown at the Provincial Exhibition winning the majority of prizes awarded for photography.

In 1897 Thompson opened a Vancouver studio and his old studio became a branch operation in the care of assistants. The Great Fire destroyed Thompson's historic studio and thousands of his glass plate negatives. In the aftermath of the fire he operated a temporary studio in the surviving Burr Block. Once the Hamley Block was reconstructed Thompson reopened a new high-class studio in a ground floor storefront, which he continued to operate until 1905.

The Vancouver studio carried on for many years. By the time of Thompson's death in 1929, he was regarded as one of the province's master photographers. •

Above: Portrait of Stephen Joseph Thompson in his New Westminster Studio. S.J. THOMPSON PHOTOGRAPH, C. 1892. NWPL 2927.
S.J. Thompson's elegant gilded photograph stamp, 1892. IHP 0203V

CHAPTER 4

A Hell of Roaring Flame

Previous page: *The most often used, and therefore most famous, photographic image of the Great Fire was taken only a few days after the event from the roof of the Burr Block looking west down Columbia Street. The composition of this image is enhanced by the small figures juxtaposed against the large-scale destruction around them. A few tents and the first temporary structures are visible near the courthouse.*

S.J. Thompson photograph, 1898. IHP 0163

Opposite page: *"Before and after" scenes of the city, taken from the same vantage point on the south bank of the river in Surrey, demonstrate the transformation of New Westminster following the Great Fire. These were sold as a souvenir set by the photographer following the disaster.*

P.L. Okamura photograph, 1898. IHP 7292, IHP 7293

othing could have prepared the citizens of New Westminster for the "Great Fire" of September 10–11, 1898. Everything seemed to conspire against the city on that fateful night. The summer had been unusually hot and dry, and it was later said that the very air on the evening of September 10 seemed as though it were flammable gas. One of the most compelling eyewitness accounts was written by an unidentified Vancouver reporter for *The Province* newspaper and published in the morning edition of September 12.[1] This article, "Gone Up In A Hell of Roaring Flame," is reprinted here, interspersed with other important aspects of the event (in italics) as recounted in an article titled "Westminster's Big Fire," from the September 17 edition of *The Columbian*, printed as an emergency sheet following the disaster.[2]

It was Saturday night in New Westminster. The clocks had chimed 11 and tired clerks had wearily packed away the goods that remained from the usual big night's shopping. All evening long the crowds had walked up and down Columbia street, laughing, chatting, buying, but before 11 the numbers had thinned out and the usual groups of young men had gathered on street corners while the occasional blue-coated policemen paraded by and cast lenient glances upon the "horse-play" in which such street corner groups are wont to indulge.

There was a dull boom on a nearby bell that startled everyone, and the word "Fire!" came instinctively to most of the listeners' lips. Almost coincident with the ringing of the bell, a bright shower of sparks was seen to rise from the riverfront near the city market building. The clatter of hose carts along the almost deserted thoroughfares and the ringing of fire gongs rapidly filled the streets again. And the size of the blaze indicated surely enough to the crowds hurrying southward that the fire was going to be a big one. The more thoughtless looked upon the prospect of a good fire with glee, but those who recognized the seriousness of the situation hurried down the sloping streets filled with the gloomiest forebodings.

Meanwhile the firemen had located the blaze in a huge pile of hay, about 200 tons in all, which was stored on Brackman-Ker's wharf. The hay was as dry as tinder for it had been there since early in the

season and the sultry summer had thoroughly prepared it for just such an important occasion as Saturday night. The nearest hydrants were located and hose lines speedily attached, but even while this was being done the whole roof of the Brackman-Ker building burst into a blaze and speedily fell in. The sternwheeler *Edgar*, which had tied up to the wharf shortly before 10 o'clock, was by this time enveloped by flames. Her cables parted and she drifted down the river on the outgoing tide a grand but awe inspiring sight …

The *Edgar* dropped rapidly down the stream but the set of the current carried her in shore and she fouled up the steamer *Gladys*, which was tied up to the wharf of the Canadian Pacific Navigation Company (CPN). Despite the early strenuous efforts of the crew and of the many volunteers, the *Gladys* took fire almost immediately. The timber and buildings of the CPN Company, dried by the fierce heat of all this summer, took fire immediately and the men on the wharf were forced to retreat or meet an awful death. The two boats now wrapped in a mad embrace of fire broke clear of the upper end of the wharf together and in a short space of time had struck the *Bon-Accord*. She, too, took flame. Her cables parted and away she went with the other two in this carnival of flame. By some strange ill-luck the waters as though in league with their fiery elements, carried the fire ships close along the wharves which line the Fraser. All were ripe for blaze and wherever the vessels touched for a few seconds there a new fire started. But all this takes longer to describe than it did to happen.

CHARLES BLOOMFIELD'S PHOTOGRAPHS, SEPTEMBER 10–11, 1898.
TOMPSON FAMILY COLLECTION

Left, top to bottom:

This first photograph documenting the beginning of the Great Fire was taken at 11:00 p.m. from the roof of the Begbie Block at Columbia and Church streets, looking down into Lytton Square. It shows that the City Market and the Brackman-Ker building on the waterfront and the cattle shed in the square are almost entirely destroyed. The outline of a few spectators can be seen leaning on the railing of the square viewing the awesome scene.

Another view of the fire as it consumes the waterfront was taken on Front Street at 11:30 p.m. from Begbie Street, where the wharves were on fire and had started to consume Fire Station No. 3 and a large coal shed.

This image of the Great Fire is taken at the critical point near midnight when "like a blast from hell … a sheet of living flame" leapt from the waterfront to the buildings of Columbia Street. The few figures of men on the street are completely eclipsed by the column of smoke and flames consuming the city. Bloomfield labelled this image "Last of the Fire Hall 11:30 p.m."

This photo taken by Bloomfield at his home on Eighth Street at midnight shows the flames rushing up the hill towards him. The silhouette of a house at the corner of Agnes and Eighth streets is visible.

Amateur Luck CHARLES ERNEST BLOOMFIELD, 1877–1954

Often by sheer luck it was the amateur photographer who captured the most compelling scenes of historic events. Such is the case of Royal City resident Charles E. Bloomfield. Born in Maidenhead, England, Charles came with his family to New Westminster in 1889. He was the youngest member of the family firm Henry Bloomfield and Sons, the first art glass company established in western Canada. Charles and his brother James were the artists who, with such expertise, crafted some of the province's finest stained and leaded art glass windows from 1890–1905.

As part of his artistic studies Charles learned the craft of photography. On the night of September 10, 1898, Charles heard the fire gong, grabbed his camera and headed downtown. At age 21 he was quick enough on his feet to reach Lytton Square just after the start of the spectacular blaze on the waterfront. He must have been excited by this opportunity to experiment with the novelty of night-time photography. He climbed the stairs to the roof of the Begbie Block to take his first photograph at 11:00 p.m.

Before his eyes, and in the lens of his camera, the fire grew to become a historic and personal disaster.

He raced down Columbia Street to the waterfront at Begbie Street and took two more images. With flames swirling in front of him, Charles witnessed the conflagration spread to the brick blocks of Columbia Street. He was likely horrified at the realization that the fire was also spreading up the hill to his family's house and business located at Eighth Street and Royal Avenue. On his climb uphill back home he took one last spectacular photograph of flames headed directly for his house.

Charles frantically tried to save his family's belongings by carrying items out into the garden to bury them under rugs and dirt. When embers from the fire landed on the Morey house next door, he climbed to the roof and emptied house plants and dirt on the flames. As he was doing this, the whole side of the house facing the fire burst into flames. Without hope of saving his house he grabbed the last of a few valuable items, including his camera and its precious glass plates with images of the fire, and found safety above Royal Avenue. The next morning he returned to take a photograph of the ashes and debris of his former home. Charles and his family decided that day to relocate to Vancouver. •

Above: Charles E. Bloomfield. F.E. EASTHOPE PHOTOGRAPH, 1896. TOMPSON FAMILY COLLECTION. **Below**: This photograph taken the morning after the fire shows the remains of the Bloomfield House and the family's famed art-glass studio, Henry Bloomfield and Sons. C.E. BLOOMFIELD PHOTOGRAPH.

Up at the Brackman-Ker wharf, where the fire had its origin, the firemen were driven from their hose by the awful heat. To their horror and amazement the pressure was exceedingly low and the mere dribble which came from the hose nozzles was little better than useless. The people in the Columbia Hotel, just across from the Brackman-Ker wharf, had speedily recognized the danger of their position and the most desperate efforts were made to save goods and effects. Lytton Square, up on which the east side of the hotel faces, was lumbered with all sorts of personal property, but the fire had spread in less than no time eastward to the city wharf and Market building. This was but a mouthful for the hungry fire devil and in an instant the Chinatown of the east end, which is on Front Street east of Lytton Square, was blazing from one end to the other.

Out on the street the scene passes adequate description. Frenzied Chinamen rushed up and down in agonies of despair. They shrieked and prayed to all the gods and devils in the Chinese mythology, but never for a moment did they cease in their struggle to save what stuff they could from their hovels and shops now rapidly being consumed. Acting Chief Watson, who

In this view of the waterfront the docks of the city have been almost entirely obliterated to reveal the old muddy banks of the Fraser.

HOWARD CHAPMAN PHOTOGRAPH, 1898. IHP 3103

in the absence of Chief Ackerman, had control of the brigade, recognized the utter futility of trying to save any of the wharves or property in that immediate vicinity. The terrible rapidity with which the conflagration spread paralyzed the brigade, which was handicapped by the miserable water supply, while private citizens could do no more than look on.

The fire, having obtained mastery of Front Street, made the first attack on Columbia by a diagonal move. The Columbia [actually named the Lytton and formerly the Caledonian] Hotel was a seething hell of flames, but the Powell Block, which adjoins it to the rear and fronts on Columbia Street was apparently uninjured. The first building on Columbia to take fire was the Bank of British Columbia block. The Chinese store of Kwong Wing Lung Co. kept the oncoming flames but a few seconds, and here the most tragic moment of the fire occurred. Mun Lee, the head of the firm, one of the wealthiest Chinese merchants in the Royal City, rushed into his store in some wild attempt to save his money. He reached his cash box but just as he grasped it he fell back dead. His corpse was carried to a place of safety and a medical man saw immediately that heart disease had been the cause of death …

A collage of the New Westminster Fire Department presents the heroes who tried in vain to save the city on the night of the Great Fire. The third fireman from the left on the top row is J.H. Watson, who served as acting chief on that fateful night.

PHOTOGRAPHER UNKNOWN, C.1897. IHP 1650

A Fraser River crane boat has recovered from the river bottom the charred hull of a vessel burned to its waterline in the fire.

Howard Chapman photograph, 1898.
IHP 3089

The Bank of British Columbia was one of the finest ... blocks and its speedy consumption was viewed with spell-bound horror by the onlookers. Opposite stood the post office and the roof of this was ablaze almost as soon as the bank was going.

All of these things had transpired so quickly that the crowd which rushed aimlessly up and down Columbia had really no idea of the extent of the conflagration. The wharves which were blazing for the full length of the city front speedily communicated with the buildings standing citywards. All up McKenzie, Lorne, Begbie, Alexander and Eighth streets the flames rushed in a mad chase. It seemed to the paralyzed citizens as though each separate street had its own particular demons, who were working in some fiendish spirit of emulation to get first to the business heart of the city. Thus it was that the whole south side of Columbia Avenue burst into flames practically at the same time. Merchants who had made desperate efforts to save such private papers as had not been put in safes or vaults were drawn from their stores in a rush for life.

The Hotel Douglas, in a corner of which the Bank of Montreal was located, became a howling volcano of flame a few minutes after it was first noticed to be on fire. The guests had ample warning though and all had escaped from the building though few had more of their belongings than what they stood up in.

It was now the dreaded wind, coaxed by alluring flames, [that] rapidly sprang into being. It came like a blast from hell full in the faces of the men who were working with the desperation of despair. A sheet of living flame swept across the street and literally burst in the windows of the splendid Hotel Guichon, the leading place of its kind in the city. The noise was deafening. Above the roar of the flames repeated explosions could be heard as the fire reached the different stocks of gunpowder, coal oil, and other explosives stored in the rich warehouses of Columbia and Front streets. The earth trembled with repeated shocks and the crash of breaking glass joined with the jar of falling walls to make the night a saturnalia horror.

Looking down the wind, the main line of the fire seemed to have proceeded in a direct line from the Market, on Lytton Square, to the handsome residence of Mr. Alex Ewen, on Begbie and Carnarvon streets. Spreading out on either side, and sweeping around the bend of the hill, it cleared everything before it ... from the burning Columbian office in the Powell building, the flames jumped to the No. 1 Fire Hall opposite. This being frame with high brick buildings on either side, it was consumed like a shingle in a stove, and the fine brick buildings in this block—the Y.M.C.A. on one side and the Duncan-McColl and Public Library buildings on the other, were fired from the rear, while St. Leonard's Hall and other buildings on Clarkson street, were soon belching forth smoke and flames. The whole heavens seemed afire, clouds of sparks and large pieces of flaming shingle being carried by the wind to alight on the clustering dwellings to the leeward, adding to the terrors of the inhabitants of that section.

How it was that many people escaped death must remain a mystery. Many hundreds found themselves cut off on Columbia Street with both sides blazing. They rushed up the side streets in a wild frenzy of excited fear and the many rumours as to deaths in the flames gained instant credence. Small mention has been made of the fire brigade at this time, but this is not because the men did not work as heroes. They fought every inch of the ground...as brave men fight, though in the full knowledge that all their efforts could do but little. In the many instances the men stuck to their feebly trickling nozzles until they were cut off and the hoses were actually burned through. The steam fire engine and the chemical were worked as never before, but in the face of such a conflagration their efforts appeared to be of as much use as a tin dipper and pail of water would have been. But even with the fate of Columbia Street sealed, people found it hard to believe that they were pitiless in their strength against the fire devil. Up, up roared the flames and the wind carried blazing pieces of wood high into the air. Still the crowd stayed downtown watching with fear stricken eyes the awful progress made by the conflagration.

Then there came the rumour that the residential portion of the city was in danger … and with the customary panic a rush was made for the upper heights. The news was too true. The myriad flying sparks had covered the sun-dried shingles and there were houses blazing everywhere. The scenes along the upper avenues and the intersecting streets beggar all description. Men and women rushed about in desperation, dragging furniture from their doomed homes. All thought of checking the progress of the flames was cast aside. Carpets were torn up, furniture was flung into the streets and all the while children ran about screaming with fright to themselves in terror of all things unknown. The broad lawns about the city hall and court house were deemed by many to be havens of refuge and these were piled high with the most wonderfully heterogeneous collection of goods and chattels. The sight was pitiful in the extreme

The once-pretty residential district surrounding the Methodist Church at Sixth and Agnes streets has been completely obliterated with the exception of a few fence posts and trees.

HOWARD CHAPMAN PHOTOGRAPH, 1898.
IHP 3095

but it was not sufficiently so to deter the malignity of the already glutted flames.

The court house that stood on Clarkson Street was not spared for an instant. It was on fire before the flames from below had even reached it, owing to the intense heat of the air and the sparks which had fallen on the roof. The records had been put into the safe but the building itself was soon a screaming hurricane. Those who had piled their furniture on the lawns made frantic efforts to get it away again. All around were blazing houses, screaming women, shouting, fighting men. And in the thick of this roaring hell with the flames above and the red hot cinders flying fast, a woman sad-eyed, pale and wan, passed through the agony of motherhood, while beside her nestled in silent fear her two children of tender years.

Street upon street fell victim to the rush of the fire. Furniture was piled up in front of houses and was burned where it was piled. The Baptist Church, the Reformed Episcopal, Holy Trinity Cathedral and the Central Methodist Church all stood within two blocks, and all were alight together. The flames made short work of the sacred edifices, indeed they seemed to roar with an increased delight as they rushed through the windows, pulled down the roofs and burst open doors in their frenzied riot.

Holy Trinity Church was reduced to nothing but its walls of granite and sandstone. A lone bell used to call parishioners was sent to the ground when its wooden support structure was incinerated.

S.J. THOMPSON PHOTOGRAPH, 1898.
IHP 8008-001

Holy Trinity Cathedral was soon left a mere outline in bare stone, and the flames, passing on, quickly enveloped the thick rows of dwellings on either side of the narrow streets, east of Sixth, and in one grand, but awful wave, swept to the west. It carried all before it here, and, spreading ever, wiped out all the clustering dwellings, the Opera House, Baptist, Methodist, and Reformed Episcopal Churches, right up to the south side of Royal Avenue, sparing only W.J. Armstrong's fine residence, here, right in the inner corner of Royal Avenue and Sixth Street.

But while the fire made rapid progress northward amid the lightly constructed dwellings, it reveled among the business blocks and factories, which, by reason of their more solid construction, gave greater opposition to the flame's desire.

The fire on Front Street, after wiping out the Market, had licked up the new cattle sheds, and, as the wind veered a point or two to the east, the heat and flames soon consumed the planking covering the outlet of the huge sewerage tunnel recently constructed beneath Columbia Street, from the ravine in which Wintemute's furniture factory was situated, to Lytton Square. Through this deep underground flume, the flames rushed a distance of ninety feet, and quickly reached several frame structures, including the factory.

The historic bells of Holy Trinity, donated by Lady Burdett-Coutts in 1861, were in storage in a shed awaiting the completion of the bell tower when the disaster struck. Damaged beyond repair, the bells were hacked to pieces by souvenir hunters in the days following the fire, then were sold as scrap by the church. One lone tenor bell did survive and hangs in the tower of the restored church.

<small>Howard Chapman photograph, 1898. ihp 3106</small>

CHURCH BELLS

The fire destroyed the city's rail connection to the CPR by almost completely burning the rail ties out from under the tracks in many places. Officials of the CPR were quick to announce their intention to rebuild following the disaster.

HOWARD CHAPMAN PHOTOGRAPH, 1898. IHP 3097

Perhaps the most remarkable scene, from a spectacular standpoint, was the burning of Wintemute's huge furniture factory, which stood at the extreme eastern limit reached by the fire ... The ravine is crossed by many bridges at these streets and the scene from these points was grand. The factory, with its big stock of oils, varnishes and dry lumber and similar flammable materials, was a rich morsel for the fat red fire. The flames poured from every window in the place until the upper stories were utterly lost in a perfect cog of flame. Every now and again a luminous detonation, followed by a burst of brighter flame in the surrounding fire would indicate the explosion of some carboy of oils. The final scene was superb. The brick and stone foundations ... appeared to give way simultaneously and the building fell into itself. The flames fairly leapt out to pierce their smoke environed prison. Millions of embers flew high into the air and that wind carried them far over the doomed city to spread further destruction among the suffering inhabitants. The ruins sunk down into a conical heap of blazing white hot ruins. Mount Vesuvius in its angriest mood could present no more awful a picture. This was the climax of the fire.

About this time, the local brigade of fire-fighters was reinforced by a part of the Vancouver Fire Department, two hose reels and a number of men, under Chief Carlisle. The latter at once proceeded to the Begbie Block, which was then to the north and east of the fire. Their arrival there was timely ... the gigantic raging billows of fire soon gutted the handsome four-storey, Begbie block. Adjoining this was the Burr block, also brick, of equal dimensions; and, alone on the

A shot of the surviving Queens Hotel and Burr Block, at the corner of Columbia and Fourth, was taken on the morning after the fire. Smoke is still rising from the downtown ashes, and furniture rescued in the panic of the night is still lying about in the middle of the street and on adjacent lots.

S.J. THOMPSON PHOTOGRAPH, SEPTEMBER 11, 1898. NWPL 236

Right, top: *Some of city hall's records miraculously survived the fire in the large brick vault that had been built to keep them safe. In the days following the fire a tent was quickly replaced by a temporary wooden city hall, built next to the remaining vault to keep the surviving records safe.*

PHOTOGRAPHER UNKNOWN, 1898. IHP 0855

Right, bottom: *A Chinese resident of the city surveys the ashes of the former Chinatown in the "Swamp," which was completely destroyed in the fire. This photograph, taken from McInnes Street, shows the view northeast up the hill to Eighth Street and Royal Avenue.*

PHOTOGRAPHER UNKNOWN, 1898. IHP 4719

Below: *Columbia Street looks barren and forlorn in this view looking east from Begbie Street.*

PHOTOGRAPHER UNKNOWN, 1898. IHP 7336

roof of this, Chief Carlisle directed operations. In this he was aided by the powerful stream of the ferry boat, which had succeeded in checking the fire, when it had consumed that portion of Chinatown east of Lytton Square. By his efforts, the Burr block, which was somewhat damaged at the rear, and the old Queen's Hotel, were saved, and now stand the only brick blocks in the city.

Away to the west, the lower portion of the city—the "swamp," where Chinatown proper and numerous small dwellings were located—had been swept bare, the water works storage shed, within the burned square, by some strange freak, being left untouched. It was a moral certainty that the electric light power house and Galbraith's and the Royal City Mills must be consumed, but the heroic efforts of all hands including the Vancouver firemen and a gang of fire-fighters from the company's mills in Vancouver, aided by a change in the wind above referred to, were successful in warding off this calamity, and the flames were prevented extending farther west than Tenth Street. They had, however, cleaned everything combustible from there to Royal Avenue, and, at the junction of these streets, had actually crossed the avenue and consumed the corner house before they were finally checked and stamped out in this direction.

Among the last houses to go were a group of large residences from the Orange Hall to Eighth Street, chief among which was that of

Sightseers take in the destruction of the Royal City on a sunny afternoon in front of the remains of the Dominion building at Sixth and Columbia streets.

P.L. Okamura photograph, 1898. IHP 0296

Mr. James Cunningham. The great width of Royal Avenue and the open space of Toronto Place alone saved the Provincial jail, although even this and other places away to the west were frequently in danger from flying embers. A second slight change in the wind which veered northward, gave ex-sherriff Armstrong's house a miraculous escape. In fact, the whole block to the east of Sixth Street, along with Royal Avenue, were considered gone at one time, and people were moving out. A well full of water saved the Murchie and Herring residences, the burning of either of which meant the destruction of another block of fine residences.

It was shortly before six o'clock on Sunday morning that the fire was "under control" … Men and women were not tired. They were simply dead beat. The murky dawn broke to find a distressed city in all the nakedness of her first grief. On all sides ruin and desolation had laid their deadly hand. The scene was appalling. In the glare of her brilliantly awful flames of the night before, the city of New Westminster was as beautiful as she had ever been, but in the fetid brown-red dawn she was ghastly, naked and dead … From the upper hills of New Westminster the sight was one never to be forgotten. Where there had been a thriving bustling city there were only smoking ruins. Not one building stood in all the vast fire swept space! Not one!

Thompson's expert eye for composition captured some compelling images of the devastation of grand buildings, such as this view of the courthouse from Columbia Street through the remains of the Curtis-Burns Block and Guichon Hotel.

GREAT WESTMINSTER FIRE. SEPT 11TH, 1898.
.1025.

THOMPSON VANCOUVER
NEW WESTMINSTER

A rare image of pulling down the remaining walls of a ruined building on Front Street.

Below: *Hardware merchant T.J. Trapp (at right) takes time to pose for a photograph with his employees amid the ruins at the site of his temporary business "block" on Columbia Street. It was a point of pride for merchants to boast that within hours of the fire they were back in business.*

The immediate concern following the fire was to house and feed the homeless of the city. The mayor organized the relief effort from the new armoury, which had received food, clothing and blankets via the tramway from generous citizens of Vancouver. As word spread across the continent, relief in various forms sped its way to the Royal City. It was said that not one house in the city closed its doors in the days following the fire so as to assist the estimated 3,000 citizens who were left homeless. The material losses were staggering, valued at over three million dollars, with only about half of that amount being insured. The loss of so many historical treasures and documents is incalculable.

The devastation led *The Province* to make this comment following its report of the fire:

> The fire determines the fate of New Westminster. Its dreams of greatness have been shattered … There will always be a community on the old site, but it will never be the community it was. It is inevitable that most of those who formerly claimed New Westminster as their home should now locate in Vancouver … the companies which were largely interested in the place will be only too glad to get their money out of it … and invested in Vancouver. But the people of Vancouver have no feelings of gratification in their hearts at this position of affairs. Their sorrow … is genuine … But … it is impossible to ignore the facts of the situation. New Westminster is a city of yesterday.[3]

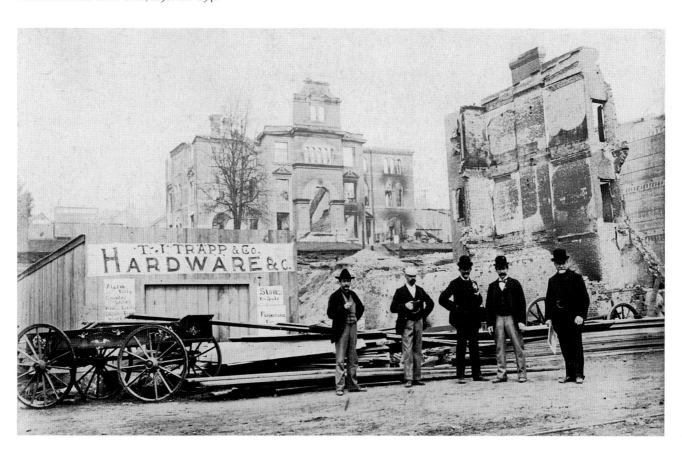

Right: *Many families left homeless by the fire found accommodation in other parts of the city or moved to Vancouver. Others built temporary homes until they could rebuild permanently. This shack was home to (left to right) Mrs. Gilchrist, Ida Birch, Stanley Birch and Mrs. Birch (in window).*

PHOTOGRAPHER UNKNOWN, 1899. IHP 0144

Below: *Without a saloon in sight, men gather instead on a stack of lumber on Columbia Street to watch the reconstruction effort.*

HOWARD CHAPMAN PHOTOGRAPH, 1898. IHP 3096

The B.C. Electric Railway Company used
an old caboose lettered with its predecessor's
initials (Westminster and Vancouver Tramway
Company) to serve as a temporary ticket office
on Columbia Street at the foot of Tenth Street.

PHOTOGRAPHER UNKNOWN, 1899. IHP 0544

Workmen attack the debris of the fire in order
that construction may begin.

PHOTOGRAPHER UNKNOWN, 1898. IHP 4718

This vulture-like viewpoint of *The Province* editors failed to take
into account the local patriotism and dedication of Royal City citizens.
Something remarkable occurred that morning following the "Great Fire"
that would forever be recounted as a mark of the spirit of the city. From
the scorched and still smoldering downtown could be heard the sounds
of the saw and hammer as businessmen and women began to rebuild
their city. The dangerous teetering walls of brick and masonry which
had not yet cooled were pulled down in the days following the disaster,
and before the dust had settled eager hands were at work stacking the
bricks in neat piles on the adjacent streets. The "city of yesterday" was
beginning to become the city of tomorrow.

City Hall Square was designated as the site for businesses to rebuild
temporary quarters. It was said that there was such a rush for building lots " … as to remind one of the early days in the gold fields." The
western end of Columbia Street too became "gay with new yellow pine
buildings and gorgeous red and blue signs painted on cotton."[4] In just
one week, more than half of the city's old stores were in business again
in temporary quarters. The city received great praise for showing its
high spirits and carrying on with the Provincial Exhibition, which was

Right: *Clerks sort through surviving records from government vaults on the burnt lawn of the courthouse. Construction of business blocks is underway in City Hall Square.*

HOWARD CHAPMAN PHOTOGRAPH, 1898. IHP 3091

Below: *The first market day following the fire was observed without delay in Lytton Square as another way to prove that the Royal City was rising from the ashes and had reason to hope for a better future.*

P.L. OKAMURA PHOTOGRAPH, 1898. IHP 4602

THE FIRST MARKET DAY AFTER THE FIRE   OKAMURA PHOTO. NEW WESTMINSTER, B.

Above: *Walker's Barber Shop boasted that it was back in business only 48 hours after the fire.*

Opposite page, top: *City Hall Square, located on Carnarvon Street between McKenzie and Lorne streets, became the temporary location for Columbia Street merchants. Its rustic buildings and canvas signs made it resemble a frontier gold-rush boom town.*

Opposite page, bottom: *The first sign of the reconstruction of Columbia Street's brick buildings, such as the Hamley Block, brought renewed hope and optimism.*

Right: *The Masonic Lodge of New Westminster, with visiting brethren from the Grand Lodge and the district, converges on the construction site of the new lodge at Columbia and Lorne streets to witness the ceremonial laying of the cornerstone.*

an unqualified success. From a city of ashes, New Westminster quickly became one of the busiest places in Canada.

Once the city was fully on the road to recovery, a citizens' committee demanded a public "Commission of Enquiry" to understand exactly what had occurred on the night of the fire—and in particular what had gone so terribly wrong with the city's water supply. The testimony was devastating. It was revealed that, in the early stages of the fire, Acting Fire Chief Watson had requested Alderman John Calbick to rush uptown to locate a water main gate and open it to connect the main hydrants of downtown to the reservoir. Calbick rushed to do as he was directed, but when he located the gate he failed to open it. In the chaos of the night, Calbick did not inform the Acting Chief. The firemen had quickly emptied the relief tank of its water and, when the water trickled from the hoses, they incorrectly supposed that the gate had been opened but the main reservoir was empty or low. The final report by Judge Eli Harrison found that the city had experimented with the water distribution system without professional engineering advice and, as a result, was left without adequate fire protection on that fateful night. ⊛

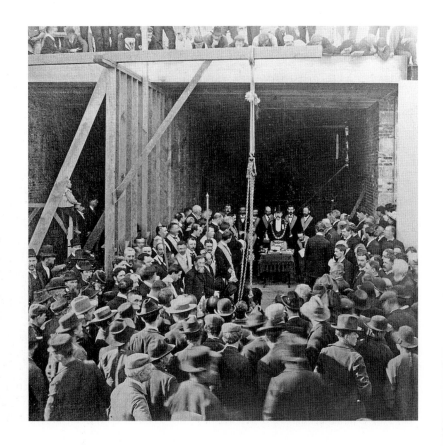

CHAPTER 5

1899–1913

Rising Like a Phoenix

Previous page: A Columbia Street panorama from Sixth Street looking west captures the city during a lazy afternoon. The buildings on the north side of the street present a continuous cover of canvas awnings to protect the stores and customers from sun and rain.

PHOTOGRAPHER UNKNOWN, 1903. IHP 0340

Designed by architect G.W. Grant to be rebuilt within its original walls, the old New Westminster Courthouse retained its dignified, if not old-fashioned, Victorian Romanesque Revival style after the Great Fire.

PHOTOGRAPHER UNKNOWN, C. 1905. IHP 0349

To outsiders, the post-fire recovery of New Westminster was nothing short of miraculous. But for the loyal and determined citizens, there was no question about the Royal City surviving and "rising like a Phoenix from the flames." Insurance funds and the sheer will of residents and businesses to get back to normal fuelled the rapid reconstruction.

New business activity, immigration to British Columbia and the improvement of the provincial economy made this period of growth a "Golden Era," one of the most spectacular and prosperous in the city's history. The strong post-fire recovery demonstrated the real economic strength of the city and its dominance over Vancouver as the centre of trade for the Fraser Valley. Construction activity in the downtown area was matched by significant new projects throughout the city in the years following the fire; one of the first expenditures of council was to rebuild the city market on its original site in Lytton Square so that its role as an important local economic engine could continue unabated.

Civic finances were put into shape, despite the losses of the fire, and residents approved a program of major civic improvements. Fire-paranoid citizens and city council ensured that the fire department saw a substantial reorganization and modernization, with new hose wagons, fire halls and a three-circuit alarm system. The problems of the much-maligned water system were immediately rectified. The reservoir was increased to a capacity of 10,000 cubic feet, with over 25,000 cubic feet per day being maintained to serve the needs of the city. Even the ferry boat *Surrey* received a huge overhaul at a cost of nearly $10,000, making it an efficient fireboat manned by a new fire-ready crew.

One year after the fire, over $700,000 had been spent on the construction of buildings. *The British Columbian*'s Fire Anniversary Issue made this report:

> ... notwithstanding the difficulties for a time in the way of obtaining necessary materials and skilled labour, Columbia Street presents an almost unbroken line of new buildings, principally of brick and stone on either side, throughout the burned district; while the fire swept hill above the business section is also adorned again with many handsome residences and pretty cottages, not to

Right: *The replacement City Market was rebuilt on its old site in Lytton Square on the waterfront, using the plans of the old building with some modifications.*

PHOTOGRAPHER UNKNOWN,
C. 1903. IHP 3735

Below: *In this rare interior photograph of the City Market, the ladies of the city can be seen swarming the tables of local farmers and merchants, looking for bargains.*

W.T. COOKSLEY PHOTOGRAPH,
C. 1904. IHP 1112

Above: *Property owners at the western end of Columbia Street were allowed to quickly rebuild wooden hotels within the fire limits in order to accommodate the homeless and new construction workers after the Great Fire. The Depot Hotel stood at the western corner of Eighth Street and Columbia opposite the CPR station.*

A. Milne photograph, c. 1900. ihp 4152

mention the new churches and halls and an elegant new Opera House … Surveying this splendid achievement of restoration work in one short year since the fire, citizens may well feel proud of the work accomplished and the substantial and handsome character of the buildings erected testify to their owners' firm faith in the city. No other city in the Province can boast of a finer line of stores, the fronts and interiors being so roomy and attractive.[1]

The cultural and civic facilities were improved considerably over their pre-fire predecessors, adding immeasurably to the overall well-being and pride of the city's residents. One of the first new buildings opened in early 1899 was the Opera House on Lorne Street. Although its outward appearance was barn-like, its interior was from all accounts "most enchanting," with artistic painting and decoration which "pleases and gladdens the eye."[2] It had seats for 1,000, with a "large dress circle and gallery for the gods" and a stage that could accommodate the scenery of any theatrical or opera company. City hall—which now incorporated

Below: *In this Columbia Street panorama the reconstruction of the city is almost completed and business has finally returned to normal. The streetcar appears to have just left the car barn and station of the new B.C. Electric Railway Company depot.* Photographer unknown, 1904. ihp 0331

The reconstruction of a new city hall on Columbia Street finally brought back some civic pride and presence to the downtown following the Great Fire. The building's architect, F.J. Bauer, very wisely incorporated a fireproof fire hall into the structure.

W.T. COOKSLEY PHOTOGRAPH, 1902. IHP 1161

a fire station—was finally rebuilt in a new Columbia Street location in 1902. The former city hall square became home to the beautiful new Carnegie Library, which opened in 1905.

The glorious architectural improvements did not diminish or disguise the city's role as a Saturday night haven for the working men of the valley. In addition to numerous city saloons, the vice district thrived in the prosperous Chinatown, rebuilt west of Eighth Street following the Great Fire. In 1903 it was estimated that 900 Chinese residents of the city conducted their lives in this ghetto that was largely controlled by wealthy Chinese merchants. Interspersed among the many upstanding businesses and homes were gambling and opium dens frequented by men and women of different races and classes.

In 1905 the dens were raided in surprise attacks by city police who, like "keystone cops," came through the front doors of many establishments only to find that the guilty had escaped through secret doors and tunnels into the maze of Chinatown's shacks and alleys. The city's prostitutes too did a brisk trade, and in 1907 there were over 30 women who occupied 24 houses "tastefully if not luxuriously furnished" on Ramage and McNeely streets. It was said that the women "flaunted in their gay attire in the street … not fit to be seen and they did not hesitate to even smoke."[3]

In this photograph taken from the waterfront, New Westminster's Chinatown, on Columbia between McInnes and McNeely streets, appears neat, orderly and respectable. In view is the substantial brick block erected by Kwong On Wo and Company, the city's largest Chinese merchant house, which imported and processed both rice and opium. Behind Chinatown's business blocks are the small homes that were the notorious bordellos of the city's "Swamp Angels."

The owners and staff of Tai Sing and Company, which operated as a butcher shop in the heart of the city's Chinatown on McInnes Street.

PHOTOGRAPHER UNKNOWN, C. 1905.
NWPL 1266

The reconstruction of the city did result in the introduction of some respectable new businesses and industries, including the $40,000 Columbia Packing and Cold Storage plant, a condensed milk factory and a new box factory in Queensborough. The city also provided some former swamp land on Twelfth Street for the B.C. Electric Railway Company tramway shops and car factory in 1902.

But these new manufacturers were a relatively small contribution to the city's economy in comparison to the phenomenal growth of its primary industrial base of lumber, fishing and agriculture. The old Royal City Mills began to increase its production, which soon included the manufacture of prefabricated housing for rail shipment to the prairies. Record salmon runs resulted in over 40 canneries operating on the river. New Westminster's shipping facilities were expanded, with the addition of several shipyards for construction and repair of riverboats. The influx of new settlers into the farmlands of the Fraser Valley also fuelled new economic activity. The production of milk, vegetables and fruit was increased and these were all transported and often processed through the city.

One of the other benefits of the new agricultural economy was seen in the success of the Provincial Exhibition of the Royal Agricultural and Industrial Society. It had grown to be recognized as one of the great fall

Workers pause for the photographer to show off their latest pride—the almost-completed interurban #1305, built at the B.C. Electric Company car shop at the foot of Twelfth Street.

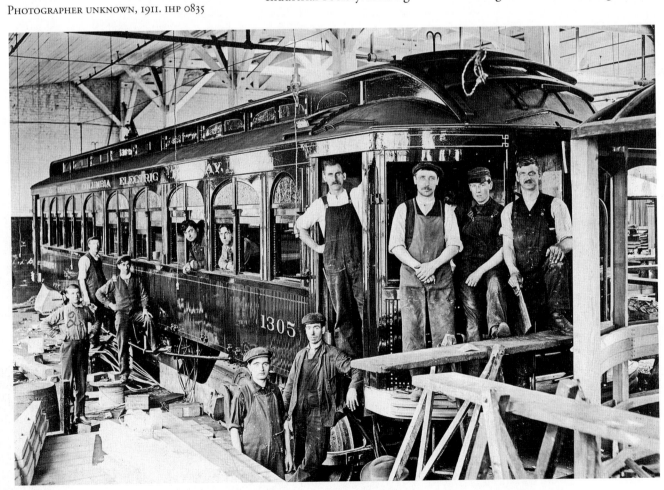

Above: *The Brunette Saw Mill in Sapperton, at the mouth of the Brunette River, was one of that community's largest employers and the location of its post office (note the sign).*

PHOTOGRAPHER UNKNOWN, C. 1908. IHP 0862

Established in the 1890s in the Glenbrook ravine behind the Provincial Hospital for the Insane, the New Westminster brickyard produced millions of bricks annually during construction booms. This photograph shows the plant's kiln where the clay bricks were fired.

PHOTOGRAPHER UNKNOWN, C. 1909. IHP 7654

This view of the Provincial Hospital for the Insane was taken from the road deck of the recently completed New Westminster Bridge. The hospital site, on the former cricket grounds of colonial days, was one of the most spectacular in the city, with beautiful gardens and views of the Fraser.

W.T. COOKSLEY PHOTOGRAPH, C. 1906. IHP 2955

The Holmes Block, built by local businessmen, was another post-fire block that created much-needed confidence for the Royal City. The ladies' fashion store operated by W.S. Collister became so successful that the block was bought by his company and renamed the Collister Block.

Wadds Brothers photograph, c. 1902. ihp 0136

Collister's store had everything a fashionable lady of New Westminster could possibly wish to purchase.

Photographer unknown, 1912. ihp 140

fairs of the country. In 1905 the province was awarded the Canadian National Exhibition along with $50,000 to fund the completion of new exhibition buildings in Queen's Park in time for this "Dominion Fair." It was "an event which is expected to advertise New Westminster and the Fraser Valley, and in fact the whole of British Columbia, more than any one occurrence of late years...All of the products of B.C. will be elaborately displayed at this great fair of the great West and … will be viewed and wondered at by thousands of visitors from the prairies and the eastern provinces."[4] The fair indeed was a success but the incessant rain dampened enthusiasm and reduced the numbers attending, resulting in a deficit.

A clear indication of the economic boom of the city was the 40 percent increase in the number of local land transactions at the city Land Registry Office. Because of Vancouver's proximity, its rapid urban and industrial expansion benefitted Royal City businesses and investors. This change was reflected in the number of residences built throughout the city. Real estate agents were quickly put to work purchasing old estates in the central part of the city and subdividing them into home building sites. New Westminster's population—which had dipped because of the recession to about 5,000 in 1898—doubled to 10,000 by 1907.

A small crowd armed with raincoats and umbrellas gathers to hear speeches on the chilly and grey opening day of the Dominion Exhibition.

S.J. THOMPSON PHOTOGRAPH, OCTOBER 1905. IHP 0085

The men of New Westminster congregate in a banquet hall of the Queens Hotel on Columbia Street to honour W.H. Keary for his efforts as the mayor of the city and as manager of the Dominion Exhibition. The guests were treated to almost endless courses of a feast and posed for this "flashlight" photograph at 9:00 p.m.

FRED L. HACKING PHOTOGRAPH, JANUARY 6, 1906. IHP 1248

It was said that New Westminster was a "City of Homes," a comment on not only the quality of houses, but the care and sophistication that was lavished on these architectural delights by citizens.

If the homes of a city are a direct reflex not only of the prosperity but the character and tastes of the community, then surely the Royal City is particularly blessed. In no city of the West can more beautiful homes be seen, and in no city in the Dominion are anything like the number of delightful dwellings in proportion to population to be seen … street after street, avenue after avenue presents but a succession of well built houses standing in emerald greens decked with the rarest blooms. The architecture is frequently concealed beneath masses of clematis, rambler roses and other beautiful creepers … The citizens of New Westminster are spending their existence in a city of gardens. Too much stress cannot be laid on the significance of this city of homes. It points to a community not only endowed with a certain degree of financial prosperity, but possessing the great quality of a love of home life and a belief in the beauty of nature. The well tended lawn, the carefully kept flower beds to be found in all quarters of the Royal City show an artistic temperament and appreciation of the opportunities and advantages of the city that makes for a contented and therefore prosperous community.[5]

The largest private home built in the downtown area as part of the post-fire reconstruction was the home of Dr. Drew at Carnarvon and Sixth streets. Designed by F.J. Bauer, the home's foundation incorporated beautifully carved sandstone blocks salvaged during the demolition of fire-ravaged downtown business blocks. When this home was demolished, the largest block, carved with the image of dragons, was rescued and moved to the New Westminster Museum.

F.E. Easthope photograph, c. 1902.
IHP 8009-01

Prosperity was also indicated by the numerous industrial plants. Although many were outside the city limits, they were connected by river, road and track to the city. This contributed to New Westminster's growth as a preferred place of residence for both employers and workers. In 1907 the city had 6 creameries, 2 tanneries, a pork-packing house, a fruit cannery and a rolling mill. There were 12 sawmills, 29 shingle mills, 3 box factories, 2 sash and door factories, a furniture veneer factory, a wooden pipe works and a factory that distilled pitch, tar and turpentine from Douglas fir. On the river was a fish-packing house and 2 cold storage plants engaged in shipping fresh fish to the eastern and European markets. Besides these natural resource industries, there were a number of other manufacturers with large payrolls: a brick works, 2 cement block factories, a distillery, a glass works, car shops, a boiler works, 2 machine works, 2 cigar factories and an aerated water factory.

New Westminster's winning spirit during this era was mirrored by its celebrated lacrosse club. Jeering rival fans from Vancouver and Victoria called the team "Salmonbellies." The Royal City fans revelled in the derogatory name, and few would have believed the hysteria that the club's success created. In 1901 the Minto Cup was established as the prize for the top senior lacrosse team in Canada. The Salmonbellies

New Westminster's fine homes and gardens were famous for their beauty. Here tea is poured on a summer afternoon at "Idlewild," the home of A.J. Hill, once located on Fourth Street and Fifth Avenue, designed by architects Samuel Maclure and Charles Clow.

PHOTOGRAPHER UNKNOWN, C. 1909. IHP 0058

Below, top: *The lacrosse "Champions of the World," New Westminster's own "Salmonbellies," pose for a photograph with the Minto Cup. Their CPR coach has stopped briefly in the Fraser Valley, en route home from their winning match with the Montreal Shamrocks to a Royal City homecoming celebration.*

W.T. Cooksley photograph, 1908. IHP 0567

Below, bottom: *Lacrosse was big business in New Westminster. In this panorama, the Queen's Park stadium is packed full of 8,000 fans watching the Minto Cup match that pitted the Salmonbellies against the Shamrocks. Imagine the thunderous applause and cheers when New Westminster won the match 13 to 5.*

Photographer unknown, July 23, 1910. IHP 1072

had no luck winning the cup until a 1908 final game in Montreal that pitted them against the famed Shamrocks, who had previously taken the prize five times. Hundreds of citizens gathered outside Columbia Street telegraph stations. When a goal was announced, the cheers could be heard across the city. After the final winning score was tapped out on the telegraph, celebrations overtook the city, attracting thousands to Columbia Street. A celebratory bonfire party stretched out into the

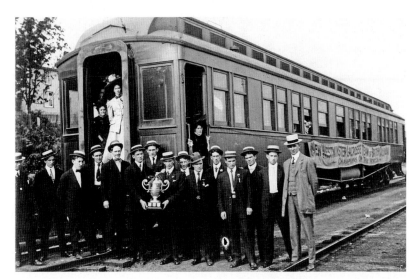

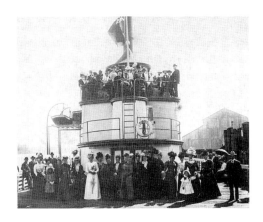

The steam ferry Surrey *was the faithful link between the city and the southern valley communities. It was not just a utilitarian ferry, but also served on occasion as an excursion boat on which the ladies of the city felt comfortable wearing their fine clothes and hats.*

<small>PHOTOGRAPHER UNKNOWN, C. 1901.</small>
<small>IHP 0952</small>

night and the boys later arrived home to a tumultuous welcome. The 'bellies became one of Canada's most celebrated sports clubs, winning the Minto Cup continuously from 1908 to 1924 with only one loss, to Vancouver in 1911.

The new and growing economy of the Fraser River port was starting to be recognized by many of the province's influential entrepreneurs, men with an economic stake in the industries located along the river. They wanted to ensure that the infrastructure to ship goods kept pace with growth, and they were assisted by the rise of New Westminster native son, Richard McBride, who became the premier of the province in 1903. At age 32 he was the youngest ever elected to the post and was so popular that he won three consecutive elections. He was said to have never failed to mention the economic potential of the Royal City in his many speeches, and his influence during the "Golden Era" for New Westminster's development was significant.

One of the New Westminster projects that McBride was able to complete was the long-dreamed-of bridge link to the United States. It finally became a reality with a million-dollar provincial expenditure and was christened with great fanfare as the New Westminster Bridge when it was declared open in 1904. The Great Northern Railway finally had its link to the Royal City and—more importantly for them—to

Below, top: *New Westminster finally saw the construction and expansion of its Fraser River docks, beginning with the unique ceremony, witnessed by a huge crowd, of the steam piledriver making a start on construction at the foot of Eighth Street.*

H.E. LEASH PHOTOGRAPH, JULY 2, 1913.
IHP 2007

Below, left: *A few brave men ride the cowcatcher of the first train over the Westminster Bridge.*

PHOTOGRAPHER UNKNOWN, JULY 23, 1904.
IHP 4645

Below, right: *The opening ceremonies of the million-dollar New Westminster Bridge marked a new era of road and rail transportation and pride in the city.*

S.J. THOMPSON PHOTOGRAPH, JULY 23, 1904.
IHP 2671

Vancouver. The bridge also opened up the trade of the valley with a permanent road link. In 1911 the B.C. Electric Railway's new interurban tramline over this bridge to Chilliwack sealed New Westminster's destiny as the hub of the valley's agricultural trade as it slowly shifted from river to rail.

Harbour improvements long sought after by the Board of Trade were finally being made with some important results. The ongoing maintenance and dredging of the river bed was finally being paid for by the federal government. This was largely accomplished through New Westminster's "Laurier Liberals" and Members of Parliament Aulay Morrison and James Kennedy. The New Westminster Pilotage Authority was established in 1906 to fund river pilots to bring ships safely to the docks. Substantial federal funding was used to dredge the river and build the first jettys at the river mouth. The construction of the Panama Canal fuelled speculation over the need for port development. The establishment of an independent Harbour Commission through lobbying by the Board of Trade was finally accomplished in 1913.

All of the industrial and business activity brought some immediate changes to New Westminster. Houses and new commercial buildings sprung up literally overnight in all parts of the city, but were especially notable in the once-sleepy sections of the West End, Sapperton and Queensborough. The city's downtown, where there were still a number of blackened building sites left by the Great Fire, saw a complete transformation. Many new concrete and brick structures filled the gaps and were outstanding architectural gems. The Dominion Trust Company built its block at Sixth Street. The city was in great need of a respectable hostelry and in 1907 E.J. Fader built the genteel Russell Hotel on Carnarvon Street. The architectural firm of Gardiner and Mercer was responsible for many of the new buildings, such as the Trapp Block, Westminster Trust Block, Courthouse addition and the Commercial Hotel. These

Top: *The building that marked the Edwardian age in New Westminster was the finely designed Westminster Trust Block at Begbie and Columbia streets, completed in 1912 by architects Gardiner and Mercer. It would reign as the city's tallest skyscraper until the 1950s.*

PHOTOGRAPHER UNKNOWN, C. 1913. IHP 1760

Bottom: *The expanding suburbs of the city led to the construction of new commercial districts and shops. The Mandeville Block, built at the corner of Twelfth Street and Sixth Avenue in 1912, was the largest commercial building outside of downtown.*

PHOTOGRAPHER UNKNOWN, C. 1913. IHP 8010-001

reflected the ideals of Edwardian permanence and sophistication. The Bank of Commerce too invested in the architectural wealth of the city by commissioning a new impressive "temple bank" by the famous architectural firm of Darling and Pearson.

The downtown's streetscape got a real modern makeover with street paving and improvements in 1910. Columbia Street was finally paved and all the double-track streetcar line's wires were placed on a line of pretty central lighting poles. A special feature was the replacement of the wooden sidewalks with beautiful concrete walks tinted "salmonbelly" pink and lined with beautifully globed cast-iron street lamps. The pinnacle of the transformation was the completion of the Westminster Trust Block, the city's first eight-storey "skyscraper," which, *The British Columbian* remarked, " ... was more than an incident in the business life of the Royal City—it marked an epoch." [6]

The Board of Trade now had a publicity department to convince everyone of the Royal City's bright future. It was headed by booster C.H. Stuart Wade. Never at a loss for words, Wade provided heady fodder in newspapers by extolling loyal enterprising citizens while scolding "growlers." Every civic statistic that demonstrated tangible growth was recounted to provide additional proof and justification. Rosy and prophetic, his shameless prose captured the spirit of the day. In one article, which appeared in the Vancouver *Province* in February 1913, Wade started with a question:

Is New Westminster's optimism justified? To obtain an answer to the query it is only necessary to ask it of the world traveled visitor who enters New Westminster. It matters not whether he be a tourist, capitalist, inventor, home seeker, manufacturer or even an ocean mariner; for the reply would be strongly affirmative. We are proud of the city; we are keen for the development of the new harbour as planned, and we at last realize that the opportune time has arrived for letting everyone ... know that the Fraser River is destined to rank with the St. Lawrence of the Atlantic, the Mersey and Thames of England, the Clyde of Scotland and it may even become the Antwerp or Hamburg of the Pacific.

New Westminster is not a city of mushroom growth, and although it may be today overshadowed by Vancouver it can claim ... attention of the great transportation companies as evidenced by the Canadian Northern transcontinental, which is actively engaged in preparing Port Mann for the completion of its Atlantic to Pacific line ... A new spirit of energy was infused about four years since; the old apathy was subjected to attack by the most enterprising of our citizens, under the leadership of our Board of Trade; the knockers or growlers were taken to task, and reinforcements backed up their efforts to impress the citizens of the many advantages we possess over other districts ... and yet there are people who still speak of New Westminster as "A place of no importance!" Possibly through ignorance (which is evidence of culpable negligence of their duty as citizens of Canada), for no man or woman who can

Top: *The new and impressive Carnegie Library was built on the old City Hall Square once it had been cleared of the former temporary shops built after the fire. Its impressive architectural design by local architect E.W. Sait would make this building a well-known and loved landmark.*

W.T. Cooksley photograph, c. 1903. IHP 0062

Bottom: *The members of the Ancient and Honourable Hyack Anvil Brigade gather on Victoria Day in front of Thomas Ovens' blacksmith shop on Eighth Street near Columbia to carry on the city's tradition of saluting the former queen with a 21-gun chorus using anvils. Note that the bystanders for this noisy event include only boys and men.*

W.T. Cooksley photograph, May 24, 1906. IHP 0063

spare a few hours and the few cents necessary to travel over the B.C. Electric railway to the Royal City would regret the trip or fail to learn something of the potentialities that are working out the great destiny of the Province of British Columbia.

New Westminster has every reason to congratulate herself in the year 1912. During the two previous years the city has been going through a re-awakening, and this last year she fully strode into the vanguard of progress in the Canadian West. Three or four years ago the city was thought of as a snug little burg with a certain number of sawmills and canneries. Today she challenges the consideration of everyone as the coming fresh water port of the Pacific coast, one of the busiest centres of industry west of Winnipeg, and a live mover commercial city from every point of view.

In 1897, 5,000 struggling people lived in the city, but today it has a thriving population of about 18,000, to whose financial needs nine separate banks with two subsidiary branches have to cater, and sixty-five active industries operating within its boundaries. Four years ago there was not a paved street, today eight miles are paved, 20 miles macadamized; forty-nine graded and 77 miles opened up. Nineteen miles of cement sidewalks have been laid and seventy-three miles of plank sidewalk. The splendid water supply from Lake Coquitlam is piped through sixty-four miles of sanitary sewers. The value of the municipal electric light plant is $350,000 and of its water system, $900,000. Its 2,050 school children attend 10 fine school buildings, valued at $375,250 and a splendid modern high school costing $100,000 is nearing completion.

All these improvements have vastly changed the appearance of the city and the erection of modern office blocks has still further thrown the town of the past into oblivion. The Westminster Trust Company opened its fine eight-storey block and another seven-storey warehouse block was put up by Mr. T.J. Trapp, a pioneer hardware merchant of New Westminster. A six-storey apartment and store building is almost completed, while plans for the coming year include a six storey building by the Dominion Trust Company, another by the *Columbian* newspaper and others by various corporations and individuals. The total permits for 1912 amounted to $1,634,528, against $1,124,587 in 1911.

All this is but an outward sign of the great manufacturing and harbour developments which are taking place. In fact it may be said that it was the publication of the harbour plans last spring which finally opened up the eyes of the world to the fact that New Westminster was not only a city with an interesting past, and an agreeable present, but also with an outstanding future. They are the only complete plans drawn on the British Columbia coast to meet the demands of the coming Panama Canal trade … and found to be worthy of the Pacific Coast and the whole Dominion of Canada.[7]

Within a few months of this article's publication even the effusive Wade would have been hard pressed to find anything good to say about the economy. The economic bubble that had led to the run of speculative development burst, leaving its victims financially devastated. ✿

Right: *With the construction completed, Columbia Street, especially at the corner of Sixth Street, presented itself as a modern and progressive place for residents and visitors to shop and do business.*

<small>Photographer unknown, 1911. IHP 8012-04</small>

Below: *The Windsor Tonsorial Parlours was located in the Windsor Hotel, with an entrance off Begbie Street. With four chairs for shaving and haircuts, it was likely a great place to hear and spread town gossip.*

<small>Photographer unknown, 1912. IHP 8020-001</small>

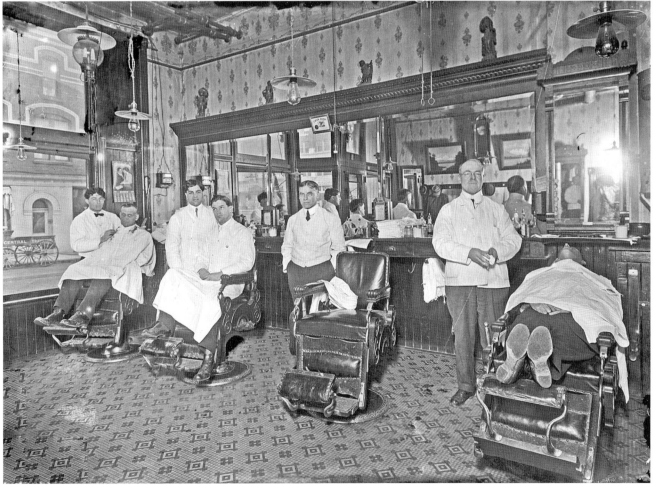

Through Japanese Eyes PAUL LOUIS OKAMURA, 1865–1937

One of the city's most remarkable early photographers was also Canada's first artist of Japanese heritage. Paul Louis Okamura, originally named Tsunenojo Oyama, was born in 1865 in Tokyo, Japan, the second son of one of the last of the country's samurai serving the Emperor's court. In order to avoid the complex rules of military conscription, he was adopted by the Okamura family to become a first-born son. In 1879 Okamura attended the Technical Fine Arts School of Tokyo Imperial University. He was a talented painter and became one of an elite artist's circle known as the Group of Eleven.

Okamura came to British Columbia in 1891 and, by chance, found a newspaper advertisement placed by St. Louis College in New Westminster seeking an art teacher. Okamura met and impressed the widely known and esteemed Oblate Augustine Dontenwill. By 1893 he was the "Professor of Drawing," leading all art instruction at the college and St. Ann's Academy. During this time he became a Catholic and acquired his name, Paul Louis.

Unable to sustain himself with the limited income his teaching position provided, he advertised that he could produce "Fine Portraits in Oil and Crayon from Photographs." Okamura's use of photographs to complete these portraits likely led to his interest in pursuing photography. In 1893 he studied photography under the guidance of a yet-unidentified Canadian photographer who taught him all of the necessary technical skills. He became the trusted assistant of the studio owner and eventually took over the operation of the business after the owner retired. Okamura took landscape photographs, with some of his best known images being those taken in the aftermath of the Great Fire.

In 1902 he built a home and studio at Royal Avenue and Fourth Street, far away from the dirt and dust of Columbia Street. Okamura was greatly assisted in his new business by all of the very influential friends he made at the college. Close to the residential district, his new studio was convenient for clients to walk to wearing their best clothes. The studio's backdrop was painted to be viewed as the parlour or hall of a wealthy home. Expensive tapestry drapes, oriental carpets, fur rugs, fine furniture and palms were all an integral part of creating an appropriate set for his middle-class clients. The studio was a tremendous success for Okamura, as it not only provided an income, but allowed him to become a respected member of the community.

One of Okamura's close friends, William H. Keary, would serve many years as a city councilor and later, from 1902–1909, as mayor of New Westminster. Keary hired Okamura to photograph the May Queen and her suite of maids in all their white floral finery from 1899 to 1920. Unlike other studio images, many of these portraits were printed on quality sepia-toned papers and demonstrate Okamura's expert eye for composition and the use of light. Okamura personally signed each one, indicating that these prints were seen by him to be a mark above the ordinary studio portrait.

Okamura attempted to relocate the photography studio to Vancouver but the recession of World War I brought him back to the Royal City to operate a storefront studio on Carnarvon Street at Begbie until 1931. He continued to work as a photographer from his old home on Royal Avenue until he died on March 26, 1937, at age 72. His passing was recognized in New Westminster with an obituary that acknowledged the valued contribution of this pioneer city photographer. •

Above: Paul Louis Okamura, self-portrait, 1906. BANNO FAMILY COLLECTION.

Top, left: Okamura's portraits of children are delightful. These cuties are Elsie and Dora Kirk, the children of prominent city residents Mr. and Mrs. H.T. Kirk. P.L. OKAMURA PHOTOGRAPH, 1902. IHP 1683. **Top, right**: Okamura's magical use of light and composition is seen in this extraordinary portrait of May Queen Miss Alvina Munn. P.L. OKAMURA PHOTOGRAPH, 1899. IHP 6911-22 **Centre**: This family picnic group is at ease in front of Okamura's camera, creating a beautiful image that he labelled "All Merry, All Happy and Bright," which captured the feeling of that golden Edwardian era. P.L. OKAMURA PHOTOGRAPH, C. 1904. IHP 853

CHAPTER 6

The Gallant City   1913–1929

Previous page: *At the open-air fete held on Columbia Street by the Ladies of the Military Hospital Auxiliary, Miss Frances Stewart was chosen by popular vote as the "most patriotic girl" in the city for her personal fundraising efforts for the war.*

CANADIAN PHOTO COMPANY POSTCARD, JUNE 9, 1917. NWPL 2892

With the collapse of the speculative boom in 1913, New Westminster's economy grew sluggish. There were some obvious signs of the recession, such as the unfinished Dominion Trust Company block on Columbia Street that workers had left after the financial collapse of the company. There were also some achievements of progress left to celebrate, including the opening of the newly paved Kingsway on September 30 when over 200 automobiles travelled into the city from Vancouver. A serious blow to the economy came with the outbreak of war in Europe. The collapse of the shipping industry caused lumber and canned salmon to pile up and agriculture production to languish. The loss of so much manpower to the war and emigration caused wage levels to drop, and there was a dramatic rise in the cost of living.

Upon the declaration of war on August 4, 1914, New Westminster immediately felt the impact, as it needed to change to accommodate the new industry of the militia. The local 104th Westminster Fusiliers of Canada was commissioned as a training unit for battalions of the Canadian Expeditionary Force (C.E.F.) and a home defense unit. The frivolity of the Provincial Exhibition was cancelled for the duration of the war and the exhibition buildings of Queen's Park became the barracks for recruits stationed in the city. Overseas recruitments began immediately, and by August 11 the "Gallant First Contingent" had been selected, with 6 officers and 144 men drawn from both the city and the Fraser Valley.

On August 22 the men marched to the B.C. Electric Railway station, where they transferred to Vancouver to board CPR trains for their long trip to the frontlines of war. On that day it was said that the air of the Royal City was " ... full of martial spirit. Flags were flying and feelings ran high ... The streets were lined with thousands of citizens who cheered and shouted fond farewells and hearty good wishes ... When the troops were finally aboard the cars and friends and relatives were allowed a few minutes to say their good-byes, the scene was one which will long remain in the memories of all. Many eyes were wet as fond mothers and wives clasped their dear ones in what they felt might be their last embrace on this earth, and the voices of strong men shook with emotion as they bade their sons godspeed."[1] In November 1914 another 7 officers and 238 men left to join the 29th Battalion C.E.F, the all-British Columbia Battalion.

In May 1915 the first reports of the fate of the Gallant First Contingent reached the city with the stunning news that the Battalion was "shattered," with 8 men reported killed and 38 wounded or missing. Citizens reeled from this, and the news continued to be devastating almost daily, with the injury and death of so many sons, husbands and friends from the city and valley. It appeared that no one was left unshaken by profound and personal grief. Every civic group and entity turned its energy towards the war effort. The city did not abandon its beloved May Day, despite the grave situation; it continued with a new patriotic theme, and the military stationed at the park formed a guard of honour for the royal suite.

The last gasp of the innocent Edwardian days of New Westminster is seen in the Armoury at a civic luncheon for the Pacific Coast Ad Men's Association.

PHOTOGRAPHER UNKNOWN, JUNE 13, 1914.
IHP 7368-139

Men bravely joined the local regiment with full knowledge of the serious dangers awaiting them at the battlefront. Twelve officers and 608 Westminster men formed the 47th Battalion C.E.F., along with many others from Vancouver. After training at Vernon, they left for the front on November 13, 1915. The Battalion, known as "The Fighting 47th," moved from its camp in England to France in August 1916 and was engaged at the Somme, Vimy Ridge (where on Easter Monday, 1917, it took part in that famous battle) and Lens and Passchendaele. The Battalion was always in the thick of the fighting and casualties were particularly heavy; 899 lost their lives and 1,718 were wounded. More than 5,300 men passed through its ranks, which had a full strength of 1,000 men. The 47th Battalion was one of the country's most famous, with many of its men receiving the highest awards and honours for bravery and service.

New Westminster even contributed women to the battlefront in the form of its nurses. In August 1914 it was reported that a number "of the fair sex" also volunteered for overseas service. The first body of women included the Misses Taylor, Lewis, Whittaker, Wiltshire and

Mrs. Burton. The Royal Columbian Hospital nursing school provided 10 of its ranks to the frontlines. Some saw service in Canadian and English military hospitals, while others were on the battlefront. Nurse Ollie Reichenbach served on the Western Front and narrowly missed being bombed in her hospital. Among the first contingent of women, Nurse Miss. E. Lewis was killed during duty.

The bravery of New Westminster's men and women on the front was matched by the determination of its citizens back home. Women led the campaign to raise funds and provide comforts to the soldiers through the Red Cross, Imperial Order of the Daughters of Empire and St. John Ambulance and Prisoners of War Society. The local branch of the Red Cross Society sent nearly a ton of linens to hospitals on the front as well as thousands of crated apples from Fraser Valley farms. Every able-bodied woman and girl in the city was armed with knitting needles and sewing machine. A tally of their work included the astounding production of 19,000 pairs of socks, 4,273 pajamas and 1,655 hospital shirts. Every conceivable way of earning funds, including garden parties and selling crabs at the city market, was undertaken and everyone contributed freely and generously. New Westminster raised an impressive $2,300,000 for the war effort over five years. The city's women were lauded by *The British Columbian* in its Victory Edition:

One thousand men of the 47th Battalion Canadian Expeditionary Force parade for inspection by Colonel Ogilvie in Moody Park.

PHOTOGRAPHER UNKNOWN, MAY 13, 1915.
IHP 671

> The noble part played by women … constitutes one of the outstanding features of the Great War. The splendid way they arose to meet the needs of the hour furnishes a spectacle which commands the grateful respect of the world. This demonstration of executive and organizing ability, down-right physical strength

Young women of the Arbuthnot Chapter of the Imperial Order of the Daughters of the Empire (IODE) are dressed in their white nursing uniforms at the open-air fete held by the Ladies of the Military Hospital Auxiliary. The event raised $7,750 for the hospital wing of the Royal Columbian.

Photographer unknown, June 9, 1917.
IHP 2644-290

and endurance, practical sympathy, patient fortitude and vigorous uncompromising patriotism has completed the emancipation of women; and has shattered the shackles of convention. The patriotism which could waive "Women's Rights" found full expression in a realm of national usefulness.[2]

The city's business community keenly supported the war effort and adapted to the terrible market conditions. Some industry was lucky enough to receive war contracts. Vulcan Iron Works, Heaps Engineering and Schaake Machine Works turned out approximately half a million shells for the Imperial Munitions Board. In order to accomplish one of the largest of the orders, the Vulcan Iron Works temporarily leased the B.C. Electric Company's idle car shops in 1916 and hired many local women to work in night and day shifts to accomplish the finishing of the shells.

The Board of Trade's industrial committee was instrumental in gaining a federal lease of Poplar Island in the middle of the Fraser River's north arm for warship building. The New Westminster Construction and Engineering Company Ltd. built a shipyard out of the bush in 30 days and even connected the island to the city with a bridge. The French government ordered four 2,800-ton wooden transport ships built: the *War Comox, War Edenshaw, War Kitimat* and *War Ewen* were all launched in 1918. At the height of its activity, the yard employed 500 men. The company received a further order to build five coal barges for France.

Despite the war effort and some local industrial growth, these years were a misery for many families. It was discovered that the wives and

Above: *The regal edifice of the Royal Columbian Hospital was a landmark that sustained Sapperton's local economy and served in part as a military hospital during and after the First World War.*

Stride Studios photograph, c. 1928. ihp 3621

Below: *The day and night shifts of the Vulcan Iron Works munitions factory, composed of both men and women, take time to pose for the camera outside the converted B.C. Electric Company Car Shops on Twelfth Street.*

C.H. Matthews photograph, 1915. ihp 7288

children of soldiers sent to the front were suffering poverty, with the meager payments from the Canadian Patriotic Fund. A local rally to financially assist the families resulted in over $25,000 being raised for the civic-operated War Relief Fund. With the first of the wounded heroes coming home in 1917, the Red Cross Society ladies spent much of their time nursing at the Casualty Unit No. 11 at Queen's Park. When it was determined that this facility would not accommodate the numbers and needs of the wounded, the ladies raised over $30,000 to equip the military wing of the Royal Columbian Hospital. It opened in 1918 and over 500 returned soldiers were nursed back to health in this facility.

In October 1918, the city suffered even more tragedy when the scourge of the Spanish flu came to B.C. Initially, the city's medical health officer, Dr. S.C. McEwen, reported only 12 cases and provided vaccination shots to anyone who wished one. One week later the situation turned deadly. The epidemic, which officials believed was confined to Vancouver, overtook the city, with over 650 cases reported. The sudden death toll of 28 caused panic. Schools and theatres were immediately closed. While restaurants stayed open, patrons were ominously urged to consume their meals quickly and get out without delay.

Civic officials banned all public gatherings and police patrolled the city in masks; they even ordered the dispersal of a Salvation Army gathering. The ladies of the Red Cross Society reacted again with competent zeal and quickly made a record 2,200 flu masks in two days and served as nurses to the ill. It was estimated that over 50 persons in the city died as a result of the epidemic.[3] The deaths were occurring so quickly among the poor and those confined to provincial institutions

Above: *Launch of the* War Comox *from Poplar Island. A lucky few guests wave atop the ship as it rides down the slip into the calm waters of the Fraser.*

CANADIAN PHOTO COMPANY POSTCARDS, 1918. IHP 7139

Below: *Poplar Island Shipyards undertook the construction of its four boats for the French government, using old-fashioned wooden boat-building technology.*

PHOTOGRAPHER UNKNOWN, 1917. IHP 1317

that the old Douglas Road cemetery on Eighth Street, which served as the potter's field, became a health menace and was ordered closed by city council for fear of contagion spreading through ground water.

Even in the midst of the flu hysteria and despair, there was no possible way the city police could prevent the unlawful assembly when news spread that the Great War was over. The news flash was telegraphed to the Royal City about 30 seconds after it reached New York on November 7, 1918, at 10:17 a.m. It was *The British Columbian* newspaper that informed the Victory Loan Office and, as it was reported:

> Within five minutes bells and whistles blared forth the message to the citizens at large … Fire Chief Watson turned out the fire apparatus, which swept through the main streets, their wailing sirens awaking the echoes. Flags broke out from thousands of windows and on flag poles in the business section, and be-flagged autos with honking horns tore loose and the crowds began to gather on Columbia Street. Within a few hours the main street was full of people as if it were evening. Enthusiasm spread and approached the pitch of delirium. A hastily formed parade of Victory girls and citizens at large, with all the flags they could lay their hands on at short notice, marched up Columbia Street and formed into a group outside City Hall. Alderman J.J. Johnston declared a public holiday and … an auto loaded with soldiers wearing the blue band of the hospital came down the street and these returned heroes were accorded a tremendous ovation … Throughout the forenoon the streets were alive with people, all expressing in many different ways their profound emotions … delirious with joy.[4]

Soldiers march on Columbia Street in what may be the official peace parade of 1918. This view is looking west from Lytton Square.

P.L. OKAMURA PHOTOGRAPH, C. 1918. IHP 4605

Above: *The capture of one of the Fraser River's giant sturgeons called for a celebratory photograph on the city's docks. With no local knowledge or appreciation of this species' rarity, conservation efforts were never considered.*

RUSSELL PHOTOGRAPH, C. 1923. IHP 2931

Below: *The Queen's Park neighbourhood achieved the air of an established suburb for the city's prominent families as a result of the grand building boom before the war. This view of Second Street, looking northeast to its intersection with Fourth Avenue, shows the impressive homes of R.J. Rickman (right) and H.C. Major. Note the curbed central boulevard installed as part of a 1913 civic beautification plan.*

PHOTOGRAPHER UNKNOWN, C. 1918. IHP 1115

The news turned out to be a bit premature, as the actual signing of the armistice did not occur until November 11. The signing launched another street celebration and a more formal civic victory parade down Columbia Street that included the men still stationed in the city.

The return of thousands of soldiers to New Westminster and the Fraser Valley in the years following the war was celebrated with great expectations, but the reality was economic stagnation. The city's population had fallen from its estimated boom high of 18,000 to an official 14,495 in the 1921 census. Citizens had formed the New Westminster Returned Soldier's Employment Committee in 1915, which did everything possible to ease men back into civic life. The committee organized vocational training, found jobs, housing, medical assistance, and even provided loans. They canvassed the city's employers to ensure that whenever a vacancy occurred a returned soldier was given preference.

In spite of these efforts the economy simply was not the same as it had been prior to the war. Many of the 286 returned soldiers who took up the offer of veteran lands for farming in 1919 found developing a "khaki farm" expensive and the market conditions bleak. Even the once-lucrative salmon-canning industry was suffering due to a complete lack of conservation enforcement and the resulting reduction in sockeye salmon. In August 1913, blasting by the Canadian Northern Railway caused a huge landslide at Hell's Gate and destroyed the major sockeye spawning run. In 1917 the sockeye run was dismal and the number of cans packed by local canneries was 75 percent below 1913 levels. By 1921 large-scale sockeye fishing was all but dead and the industry began to exploit other species.

Above: *Crowds enjoy the midway and carnival of the Provincial Exhibition.*

Photographer unknown, 1928. IHP 7272

Below: *The sale of ladies' fashions surged following the Great War. This beautiful display is in the window of the T.H. Smith store on Columbia Street.*

Photographer unknown, 1918. IHP 0112

In the face of these hardships, the old spirit of the Royal City returned with the 1919 Provincial Exhibition. With the soldier's training camp removed from the park, the Royal Agricultural and Industrial Society expanded the exhibition buildings and prepared for the fiftieth anniversary of the fair. Mild hysteria broke out in the city with the news that the Prince of Wales would honour the city with a visit to open the exhibition to the public. The extensive preparations for this event included arches of welcome and a long line of Great War veterans in the park. When the Prince arrived in the city on September 29, thousands lined the route from Kingsway in Burnaby. Once the Prince's automobile cavalcade reached Columbia Street the crowd broke into "tumultuous acclaim, which ran up the line like fire through prairie grass." [5] Over 22,000 people entered the gates that day, and during the week the fair saw over 90,000 visitors. The fair was back and was a stunning success.

Many citizens would toast the arrival of the Prince with a celebratory drink. Despite Prohibition, which had come to British Columbia on October 1, 1917, there was still plenty of booze available for those who knew where to find it. Some of the city's hotel bars closed, while others served the legal "non-tox," or beer with low alcohol content, over the counter and secretly supplied the good illicit stuff under the counter. The Westminster Brewery survived by producing that swill beer with 1.5 percent alcohol popularly known as "beaver piss." You could get whisky if you could convince your doctor to prescribe it for medicinal purposes. The people of the city were apparently in such "poor health" that the idle B.C. Distillery in Sapperton reopened in 1918, just to keep up with the thousands of prescriptions. Rum runners from the U.S. also did a

brisk business, as did local Chinese firms, many of which managed to avoid scrutiny and import "Tiger Whisky" to fill the large demand.

Finally, with the end of the war, Prohibition was rescinded in favour of moderation and the first Government Liquor Store opened in the Burr Block on Columbia Street on June 15, 1921. The first buyer in line was a Seattle resident, who was eager to get his hands on the "hard stuff" now that the American Prohibition was in effect. Locals seemed wary of paying a permit fee of 50 cents to the government and some said they would rather keep purchasing their liquor from cheaper, more reliable bootleggers. A booming rum-running business soon began from the city's ports, with fishing boats loaded to fill an insatiable thirst in Washington State for Canadian whisky and spirits.

On October 27–28, 1921, a heavy rainstorm hit the Fraser Valley. The practice of logging and burning at the Coquitlam Lake watershed had denuded its steep slopes, resulting in an accelerated rate of run-off. The lake over those two days rose at the rate of 6 inches an hour; at one point the water was over 9 feet 6 inches deep at the dam spillway, allowing for a phenomenal flood event to occur. The water raced through the Coquitlam River valley in a raging torrent, tearing out steep banks and

The city's war memorial, built from funds raised by citizens, was dedicated at "Leopold Place" at the corner of McBride Boulevard and Columbia Street in 1922.

C.E. STRIDE PHOTOGRAPH, NOVEMBER 11, 1922. NWPL 3141

Above: *The Gyro Auto Camp attracted tourists who were travelling with tents in their cars from the United States over the Pacific Highway. It was located in Queen's Park near the exhibition buildings and still survives in part today as part of the Parks Department work yard.*

PHOTOGRAPHER UNKNOWN, C. 1928. IHP 8017-02

Below: *The C.C. Brown automobile showroom at the eastern end of Columbia Street was just one of the many new dealers in town keeping up with sales in the new-found craze for cars.*
STRIDE STUDIOS PHOTOGRAPH, C.1928.
IHP 8018-003

finding a new path on the valley's road, which was quickly destroyed. New Westminster's water mains were torn from their precarious trestles and ripped to pieces; in some places they were buried under tons of debris.

With New Westminster's water supply system destroyed, an emergency meeting of city officials was called to deal with the crisis. The city was totally dependant on Coquitlam Lake, with no alternative sources other than the reservoir. With a normal daily consumption of 2 million gallons, the reservoir supply was estimated at only 300,000 gallons, which would last only two and a half days with severe restrictions. *The British Columbian* went to press on Monday, October 31, 1921, with an extra-edition headline: "WATER FAMINE THREATENS—City Faces a Calamity Second Only to the Great Fire." Emergency water restrictions were put in place, old ground wells were put to use and extra fire pumpers stationed in the city in case of fire. With the permission of the Municipality of Burnaby, city works crews raced to tap into their mains. Burnaby received its water from the Seymour Mountain reservoir, which provided an ample supply to fill the city's needs, averting a full-scale crisis.

The year 1922 was marked by the city's completion of its cenotaph to the Great War. The project had been initiated by the Board of Trade, which received so much support across the city and district that an original bronze life-size statue of a soldier on an impressive monumental granite base could be funded. The sculpture was the work of a B.C. soldier, George Paterson, who worked in concert with an Italian sculptor, A. Fabri of Vancouver. Dedicated on Armistice Day, November 11, 1922, the cenotaph's statue was unveiled by Brigadier General Victor W. Odlum before a crowd of 7,000 at Leopold Place on Columbia Street and McBride Boulevard, overlooking the Fraser. A civic "Roll of Honour" was read of the 239 men and 1 nurse who died during duty.

One of the great changes to the city in this era was wrought by the crazed enthusiasm for the private automobile. *The British Columbian* even printed a special automobile section every Saturday to feed the fever. Thousands of new cars were on the road and New Westminster accepted the new industry with open arms. At the eastern end of Columbia Street a long line of competing auto showrooms opened to sell the latest models. Driving was seen as a fun sporting activity that was full of adventure. British Columbia was the last place in North America still driving on the left. The "rules of the road" changed on January 1, 1922, and driving on the right-hand side of the road was now encouraged. People were outraged, however, after the Municipality of Burnaby painted a centre line down Kingsway and police actually handed out tickets to offenders who crossed the line.

New Westminster was the home base of the Good Roads League, which advocated for better road surfaces, signs and highways. One of the road projects, projected as early as 1910, was the construction of a Pacific Highway to connect the province with the western U.S. states. As part of this plan, New Westminster residents were prime movers behind the Peace Arch, which was completed in 1921. Finally, the province spent almost a million dollars to pave the Canadian section of the new Pacific Highway, which opened on September 3, 1923. Cloverdale was chosen as the location for the celebration and after speeches and dinner, the city's 47th Battalion Band played and there was dancing under the moonlight on the pavement of the highway.

Many young women in the 1920s cut their hair in the popular bobbed style and found employment and a certain sense of freedom. Pictured here are women employed with B.C. Telephone in the Westminster Exchange as "Hello Girls," watched over in the "operating room" by supervisors who stand in position at their various stations.

Photographer unknown, 1927. IHP 5663

In this publicity photograph staged inside the Westminster Paper plant to convey its sanitary packaging conditions, women workers don white uniforms to pack Purex toilet paper.
PHOTOGRAPHER UNKNOWN, C. 1927. IHP 7626

The industrial boom of the 1920s saw the construction of the Triangle Chemical Company and Westminster Paper Mills on the north arm of the Fraser River. The paper mill was destroyed by fire in 1929, but the plant was rebuilt and grew to become the Scott Paper plant.
PHOTOGRAPHER UNKNOWN, C. 1927. IHP 7374

Automobiles could now travel from the U.S., drive over the New Westminster Bridge and along Columbia Street and connect with Vancouver via Twelfth Street and Kingsway. The city was invaded by American tourists on holiday car-touring vacations. The New Westminster Bridge would soon have over a million automobile crossings annually; on July 2, 1928, a record 12,972 cars made the short run across the Fraser. The Gyro Auto Camp was built to accommodate the auto camping tourists in Queen's Park and was a great addition for the city's economy.

By the mid-1920s the pace of industry and business quickened and New Westminster was finally back on the road to prosperity. One of the clear indications of the new economy was significant new industrial and port growth. In Sapperton, the Canada Western Cordage Factory opened in 1921, adding jobs to the local economy and millions of feet of rope to both local and export markets. In the west end of the city the north arm of the Fraser River became the favored location for the Triangle Chemical Company, a Kraft Cheese Box factory and the Westminster Paper Mills. A waterfront parcel at the foot of Tenth Street became the new home of the Fraser River Dock and Stevedoring Company in 1924 and the Brackman-Ker Milling Company Ltd. doubled its capacity to handle new grain shipments from the prairies.

Even Columbia Street, which had not seen a substantial architectural landmark built in years, was suddenly making a comeback. One of the new developments began with a fire on August 17, 1925, that destroyed the waterfront City Market at Lytton Square. Rather than rebuild at the

Below, top: *The City Market's interior decor was as utilitarian as a barn, but as a popular shopping place for inexpensive and quality products of the Fraser Valley, it was long regarded as one of New Westminster's greatest assets.*

PHOTOGRAPHER UNKNOWN, C. 1927. IHP 3737

Below, bottom: *Opening day of the new City Market on Columbia Street heralded a new era for district farmers and local shoppers.*

PHOTOGRAPHER UNKNOWN, APRIL 30, 1926. IHP 3736

old location, council chose to reconstruct the building within the old market square and situate the building with a convenient storefront on Columbia Street. With insurance funds and voter's approval for a civic bylaw that raised the needed $70,000, "the finest market yet established in the province" was constructed.[6] It was opened on April 30, 1926, by Mayor Annandale and the Honorable E.D. Barrow, Minister of Agriculture, in a fitting ceremony that once again reinforced the Royal City's position as the centre of trade for the farmers of the Fraser Valley.

The commercial activity of Columbia Street prompted local investors to build a new vaudeville and movie theatre on the long-vacant ravine lot adjacent to the Bank of Commerce. The city had been without a place for amusement since the old opera house was condemned and finally demolished in 1926. The Edison and Royal theatres were nothing more than converted stores, lacking any pretension. Investors raised $100,000 and Famous Players Canadian Corporation leased the property and contributed another $50,000. The Columbia Theatre opened with great ceremony in 1927, marking a new era in the cultural history of the city. Designed as a true movie and vaudeville palace, it was decorated as an "atmospheric theatre," the Moorish style of its exterior carried throughout the interior "with an effect that leads one to believe that he or she is seated in an open garden."[7]

New Westminster's building inspector was leading the way to redevelop the city, in spite of some reluctant property owners. City council had long wished to be rid of Chinatown's vice section. Gambling

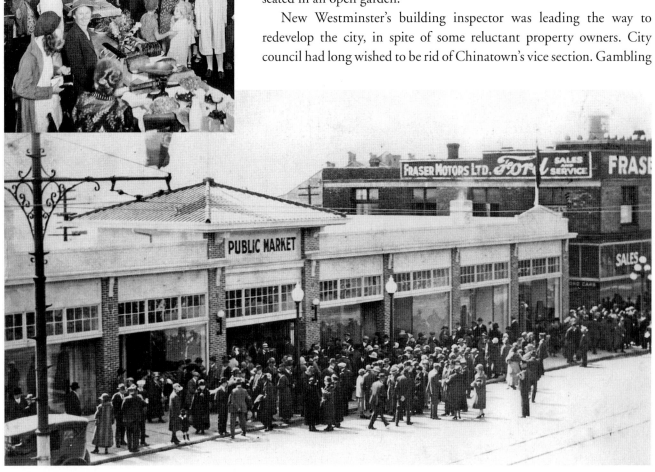

was still a big problem, and it only grew larger with the police "crackdowns" in Vancouver. Chinese merchants there put their "high-rollers" into limousines and spirited them away to New Westminster for big games to avoid disruption by raids. The city took action by ordering the demolition of blocks of buildings that comprised the homes of many Chinese and Japanese businesses at the eastern end of Columbia. This displacement led many residents to move further east, creating another Chinatown. Much of the former Chinatown became new building sites for automobile showrooms and repair garages. However, some Asian business owners refused to move and instead rebuilt their stores and took advantage of the business boom.

Throughout the 1920s, the value of residential construction increased steadily, mirroring the growth of the local economy. New Westminster's policy of not taxing improvements provided a substantial incentive to build with quality. Total permit values rose from $108,000 in 1918 to nearly $2 million in 1928, of which $308,000 alone was for residences. From 1927 to 1929 over 500 homes were built throughout the city during this bungalow boom. It was said that "New Westminster has always been a city of attractive homes, a city in which pride of home

The West End neighbourhood was the popular location for middle-class homes. In the years following the war it was the scene of a "Bungalow Boom." This photograph of Dublin Street looks east to its intersection with Tenth Street.

Stride Studios photograph, c. 1925. ihp 8019-01

The Columbia Theatre was a marvellous addition to the city, finally providing a first-class theatre for both vaudeville and movies. It was one of the first true atmospheric theatres in Canada and was decorated by artist John Girvan in the style of a Spanish courtyard garden.

Leonard Frank photograph, 1928. Burr Centre for the Performing Arts collection

Opposite page, top: *The Women's Building is engulfed in flames from the fateful fire that destroyed the buildings of the Provincial Exhibition.*

PHOTOGRAPHER UNKNOWN, JULY 14, 1929. IHP 356

Opposite page, centre: *Sir Winston Churchill is escorted by Colonel A.L. Coote in an inspection of veterans of the Great War at the Diamond Jubilee of the last Provincial Exhibition held in Queen's Park.*

STRIDE STUDIOS PHOTOGRAPH, SEPTEMBER 2, 1929. NWPL 2149

Below: *A panorama of the incredible Provincial Exhibition buildings of Queen's Park, taken from the reservoir shortly before the buildings were destroyed by fire.*

STRIDE STUDIOS PHOTOGRAPH, C. 1928. IHP 1492

was demonstrated in well-kept streets, unanimity in flower gardens, and a high standard generally in neatness and attractiveness of its residential areas. Today New Westminster is outdoing its own record in the model type of homes which are rapidly filling the vacant lots in the residential areas and pushing ever wider the boundaries of these districts." [8] Through the firms of the Westminster Trust Company and A.W. McLeod Ltd. families were able to secure building loans necessary for small wage earners to own their own castles.

The old Royal City Mills site, an 18-acre waterfront parcel at the west end of the city centre, had been idle since its 1913 fire. The site was purchased in 1927 by Pacific Coast Terminals, a company composed of local capitalists led by Valentine Quinn. Their 2.25-million-dollar investment saw the construction of conventional terminals, a huge cold storage plant and modern mechanical cranes connected by road, rail and wharf. This development transformed the city's waterfront and finally fulfilled the dreams of the Board of Trade for first-class port facilities. The Panama Canal was finally being exploited as a trade route for British Columbia's exports and this, coupled with the growing Asian markets, caused the port of New Westminster to boom. From a mere 13 cargo ships calling in at port in 1921, the number of ships gradually grew until, by 1930, 297 ships took on 40,000 tons of cargo worth over 12 million dollars.

In 1929 the city was preparing to celebrate 60 years of the Provincial Exhibition with a huge Diamond Jubilee celebration. Sir Winston

Churchill and Premier Tolmie were to be on hand to open this very special fair the same day as opening the Pacific Coast Terminals. However, tragedy struck the city again in the form of fire. On July 13 the new plant of the Westminster Paper Mills on the waterfront was destroyed in a million-dollar blaze. The next morning at six o'clock, exhausted fire crews received a new alarm that the exhibition buildings in Queen's Park were on fire. The wooden buildings were a mass of flames by the time the crews arrived, with the flames spreading so quickly they even threatened to spread to the residential area across from the park. Low water pressure from the hydrants hampered the crew's efforts so that, within an hour and a half, the great exhibition buildings were reduced to a pile of ashes. Everything was destroyed but the cattle sheds, banquet hall and the old fisheries building, then in use as an administration building.

Once again the spirit of New Westminster was remarkable. The directors of the Royal Agricultural and Industrial Society met and immediately decided to carry on with the fair. Vancouver was quick to offer its exhibition halls at Hastings Park for the event, but civic pride refused the offer; after the provincial government pledged $15,000 and surrounding communities provided other funds, the exhibition was on. There was no time to rebuild so the idea of a fair under tents became the novel solution.

The great fair opened on Labour Day, September 2, 1929, as planned and the presence of the Right Honourable Winston Churchill, the great

British statesman, drew crowds in record numbers. The great assembly of 37,000 smashed the old record set by the Prince of Wales. Churchill inspected a column of veterans and stood before the crowd to give an "eloquent address worthy of his reputation": "You have come through fire and I admire the courage and resource of those in charge, which has been such that not even the heavy blow you have sustained has been able to mar the success of your undertaking. It is a good sign ... perseverance and dogged courage that does not know defeat, typical of the British race." [9] Sadly, this was the last Provincial Exhibition ever staged in the city.

At the Pacific Coast Terminals another ceremony marked the revolutionary change of the city's waterfront brought by the construction of the cold storage plant. There was pageantry from the past in the form of a costumed canoe paddler representing Simon Fraser who paddled with his voyageurs to the docks with the official key used by May Queen Frances Schnoter to open the plant. As the door opened, airplanes flew overhead, bombs (fireworks) were sent up, flags were raised and the band played the national anthem. The whole ceremony was broadcast live on the terminal's newly opened radio station. It closed with local and Washington State native bands dancing on the docks and competing in canoe races. The city was ready for a new era as one of the country's largest sea ports. ✿

Right: *Native canoes get ready to race on the Fraser River at the opening of the Pacific Coast Terminals.*

H.G. Cox photograph, September 2, 1929. H.G. Cox collection, courtesy Susan Hopkins

Below: *This panorama of the city shows off the success of the port with its full harbour of visiting cargo ships.*

Stride Studios photograph, c. 1929. IHP 2321

S. S. MADRAS CITY

S. S. TROUTPOOL

Right: *A rare early aerial view of New Westminster taken over Queensborough shows the new Pacific Coast Terminals under construction.*

Below: *Ships unloaded and received cargo at the new Pacific Coast Terminals.*

S. S. QUEBEC CITY

S. S. SHEAFSPEAR

Pictorialist Partners John Vanderpant, 1884–1939; Horace G. Cox, 1885–1972

Our Royal City was home to John Vanderpant and H.G. Cox, two of Canada's pre-eminent art photographers. Born in Alkmaar, Netherlands, in 1884, John Vanderpant came to Canada and made his home in New Westminster, where he operated a commercial photographic studio from 1919–1927. Horace Gordon Cox was born in England in 1885 and attended the Kiddminster School of Art before immigrating to Canada in 1908. He settled in the Royal City in 1911, working initially as a draughtsman with the B.C. Electric Railway Company and later for the B.C. Department of Public Works. Unlike Vanderpant, Cox chose to pursue his art photography as a part-time endeavour.

Shortly after the arrival of Vanderpant in 1919, the two men met and became close friends, sharing a keen interest in art and photography. At this time the world of art photography was gaining many converts. A network of clubs, journals and salons was being established both locally and internationally. Vanderpant and Cox identified with the Pictorialist style of art photography that had grown out of the Arts and Crafts movement. "Pictorialists" distinguished themselves as artists using the medium of photography. They intended to evoke the painting style of nineteenth-century European romantic artists with their misty portraits and landscapes. Pictorialist photographers utilized devices such as balanced composition, soft focus, and the play of light.

Vanderpant assumed control of the art exhibits of the Royal Agricultural and Industrial Society's Provincial Exhibition in 1920. Under his leadership, National Gallery of Canada loan exhibits came to town including works of the Group of Seven. In 1921 the first New Westminster "International Salon of Pictorialist Photography" was organized as part of the art exhibits, and the photographs of Cox and Vanderpant figured prominently alongside many of the international photographers they admired.

Vanderpant soon grew dissatisfied with the direction of his work and became an outspoken critic of Pictorialism, venturing instead into the world of modernism. He moved his studio to Vancouver in 1927 and aligned himself with avant garde artists such as Group of Seven painter Frederick Varley. Vanderpant challenged convention and began anew. He produced stunning works of art, taking photographs of grain elevators and closeup images of cabbages cut through the middle. Although the reaction to his work was often hostile on the staid salon circuit, Vanderpant persisted and left a lasting legacy as a pioneer photographic artist.

Cox continued to support Pictorialism for many years despite his friend's aversion. By 1939, however, he too had veered into new territory with his own Vancouver Art Gallery exhibit "The Book of Muriel," composed entirely of images of one nude model. During his part-time career as a photographic artist from 1924–1940 his work received acclaim on four continents in many prestigious exhibitions. Cox would have largely been forgotten if it was not for his great-granddaughter, Susan Hopkins, who rediscovered his collection languishing in storage. In 2004 his work was the basis for an exhibition titled "Athens on the Fraser—The Photographs of H.G. Cox," held at Presentation House in North Vancouver and curated by Bill Jeffries. •

Opposite page, clockwise from top left: View of the government docks and fishing boats at the foot of Eighth Street on the Fraser River. This photo, titled "At Anchor," epitomizes the Pictorialist style and love of shadow and light. H.G. Cox, c. 1930. H.G. Cox collection, courtesy Cox family. A portrait of New Westminster May Day Maid of Honour Dorothy Alcock. Vanderpant Studio, 1925. IHP 6911-106. Art exhibit at the Provincial Exhibition. John Vanderpant photograph, 1920. Author's collection. Titled "May Day," this delightful view is of an unidentified costumed flower girl peeking through the impressive doors of the post office on Columbia Street. H.G. Cox, c. 1927. H.G. Cox collection, courtesy Susan Hopkins.

CHAPTER 7

1929–1945

Perseverance and Dogged Courage

Previous page: *With no safety harnesses in sight, these steelworkers join the first beam to connect the Pattullo Bridge across the Fraser River.*

H.G. Cox photograph, 1937. (Reprinted from original negative) H.G. Cox collection, courtesy Susan Hopkins.

Opposite page, top: *This image, taken on a wet day from atop the Westminster Trust Block looking west to the docks of Pacific Coast Terminals, seems to capture the bleak mood of the Great Depression in New Westminster.*

Stride Studios photograph, c. 1932. IHP 7791C

Opposite page, bottom: *Columbia Street, despite the economic uncertainty of the era, always seemed busy with shopping and commerce. This image was taken in front of the Westminster Trust Block at Begbie Street, looking east. Note the Pacific Highway's directional sign and the street lamps decorated with Christmas trees.*

Stride Studios photograph, c. 1935. IHP 8000-003

Initially, the stock market crash of October 29, 1929, and the troubles of Wall Street seemed far away. Other than a few newspaper reports the economic impact was hardly noticed in New Westminster. The new harbour terminal and the success of the Diamond Jubilee exhibition inspired great hope for the future. The construction boom was still transforming the city and the weekly building pages in *The British Columbian* were filled with descriptions of new building projects. Even the disastrous fires of the summer of 1929 led to new construction. Insurance funds from the exhibition building fire provided the city with the opportunity to construct a new multi-purpose arena for use as a new civic auditorium and sports facility. The Westminster Paper Company even rebuilt a much larger plant on its former site at a cost of $750,000.

However, it would take the city's noted "perseverance and dogged courage", as described by Winston Churchill, to survive the challenges that lay ahead. Eventually the stock market crash would have a devastating effect on the international markets for the city's agricultural, fishing and lumber industries and the new exporting facilities of the Pacific Coast Terminals. It was not until May of 1930, with building permits beginning to fall off and industrial plants suffering from the slowdown, that the reality of the "Great Depression" began to set in for many city residents. The lumber industry was one of the first casualties and, in 1931, sawmill workers were faced with wage rollbacks as high as 40 percent. At Fraser Mills, workers launched a strike that would last several months, until they had no choice but to accept wages that were much reduced. Then in 1932 the Brunette Lumber Company suffered a fire which caused $95,000 in damage. The mill never recovered and Sapperton was severely impacted, with a loss of residents and commercial activity. Many workers were forced to leave their rental housing and live in self-made shacks, forming squatters' villages along the riverbank in Sapperton and Fraser Mills.

City council and business owners were nervous about the number of jobless men from across Canada flooding into Vancouver and finding their way to the Royal City. The unemployed masses were seen as a destabilizing influence to an increasingly insular city that very much feared the "reds" that were marching and rioting in Vancouver's streets.

Above: *A view of Sapperton taken from the wall of the B.C. Penitentiary looking northeast over Cumberland Street and the Fraser Cemetery shows the rural character and undeveloped lands that still existed in parts of the city.*

The economic devastation some families were experiencing was evident in the large number of properties being lost by their owners to the city for the non-payment of taxes. In some cases, rather than renting the properties to needy families or reselling them, council ordered the city engineer to demolish large old vacant homes for fear they would offer harbourage to indigents. The fear was purely economic, as any person, after establishing their residence, would qualify for civic payment of relief (welfare) funds. The houses were also considered "white elephants" because of their size and cost to maintain. The added benefit in city council's eyes was that the building sites would create construction jobs.

Unfortunately this policy led to some of New Westminster's most historic and architecturally significant homes being demolished. Even the 1861 J.A.K. Homer House at 211 Columbia Street was not saved, despite its position as the oldest house in the city and the good condition of its imported California Redwood siding. The Fisher mansion at Seventh Street and Third Avenue, designed by Samuel Maclure and Richard Sharp in 1891, was an outstanding masterpiece of the Queen Anne style and it, too, was wastefully demolished for salvage and the lots created. One of the most regrettable casualties of this program was Columbian College, housed in the massive 1891 H.V. Edmonds mansion,

"Blossom Grove," on First Street and Queens Avenue. The Depression hit the college hard and it was closed in 1936 and leased briefly as Towers College until the non-payment of taxes made it the property of the city. Council waited for nothing, ordering its demolition and the creation of lots on prestigious Queens Avenue for sale in 1939. They remained unsold until the city finally discounted them, practically giving them away to well-off buyers and builders.

The long-feared labour unrest posed by "reds" came in June 1935 when New Westminster's hundreds of dock workers joined, in sympathy, a strike of the Vancouver and District Waterfront Workers. The port

Right: *The city's insurance on the Provincial Exhibition buildings that had been destroyed by fire funded the construction of the Queen's Park Arena. Intended as a civic auditorium, it became more famously used as a sports arena for hockey and box lacrosse.*

LEONARD FRANK PHOTOGRAPH, C.1935. NWLP 1226

Below: *A panorama of Columbian College on First Street and Queens Avenue shows the size and good condition of the buildings demolished by order of city council during the Great Depression.*

STRIDE STUDIOS PHOTOGRAPH, C. 1935. IHP 8018-001

A view of the docks and shipping facilities at the Pacific Coast Terminals shows how beautifully it integrated road, rail and river.

was shut down by dock workers' pickets. Local business and civic leaders created a management-friendly Royal City Waterfront Workers Association in opposition to the union and rehired 350 new and old workers. Rather than have the new workers face the daily onslaught of the picket line, a boarding house was created on the docks to keep the hundreds of replacement workers on shift and cargo moving. The reaction on the part of the strikers was predictable. Acts of violence started to erupt across the city and soon escalated into what was described by *The British Columbian* as a "miniature reign of terror," one of the most compelling events to ever occur in the city.[1]

The first incidents of violence were a regular part of the picket line at the dock entrances. Along Columbia Street fist fights and verbal attacks between "strikebreakers" and "strikers" became common. By July a menacing atmosphere pervaded the city as several of the strikebreakers and their families found threatening notes left on their doorsteps. One note read: "Have that scab husband home tonight … If you don't you and kids will take the result. Beware. Midnight." Another family awoke to find a cross burning on their lawn and a note signed "K.K.K."[2]

Events became even more serious in the form of the burning of a dock worker's house in Port Mann. In Sapperton a strikebreaker used a gun to fire a shot and chase away a group of men who had entered his house in the night. Another strikebreaker's city home was set ablaze with oil-soaked rags; fortunately, it was quickly put out by the fire department. The city was now in a state of high anxiety, with front-page headlines about the strike almost daily. A small cabin located on the north arm waterfront, home to a strikebreaker, was completely destroyed by fire a few days later. In August there were finally arrests and charges laid in some of the arson attacks and tensions seemed to reduce considerably.

These incidents did not assist the cause of law-abiding strikers who had tried to make their grievances through the normal channels of labour negotiation. The men on strike had made applications for relief to the city but soon found that no sympathy existed for their cause. Council was quite indignant that the strikers had chosen to disrupt the civic picnic party in celebration of the city's 75th Anniversary and reminded strikers that it was against provincial statute for city council to use relief funds provided by the province to assist striking men or their destitute families. Other labour unions too were restless at council's complicity in supporting shipping management and allowing provincial police to patrol the docks.

Just when the strikers began to negotiate again with shipping interests and the federal government, more violence erupted on the docks. The morning arrival of strikebreakers was met by a crowd of strikers and many of their supporters from Vancouver. The cars entering the docks were pelted with stones, terrifying the occupants, breaking some headlights and sending city police into action. The dispersal of the crowd was ordered by the Chief of Police, who had his men and provincial police from the docks disperse the crowd using their batons. Men who did not move quickly enough were "tapped on the head or prodded" and 14 of the strikers and supporters were arrested. The Chief of Police ordered the end to further pickets and the striker's camps at the dock gates were removed. Eventually, most of the workers had no choice but to return to work, as the strike had been broken.

Surprisingly, despite the many hardships of the era, the Royal City did not suffer unduly through the Depression years. Many of the city's employed residents saw their standard of living improve as prices fell faster than wages. By 1936 the worst of the Depression seemed to be over; export markets returned and the city was enjoying a remarkable increase in port activity and general prosperity. The unemployed were assisted by the creation of a number of civic works projects designed to employ city men on relief. The largest of these was the development of Hume Park, which was carved out of the bush on the banks of the Brunette

Because the transfer of cargo on New Westminster's docks was one of the city's major economic generators, management and city council did everything in their power to quash a strike of longshoremen.

STRIDE STUDIOS PHOTOGRAPH, C. 1938. IHP 1652

River by the parks board. The park was named after the popular mayor, Fred Hume, who did so much to lead the city through hard times. He was also a talented horticulturalist who advocated the beautification of the city through the development of its parks and gardens.

The return to prosperity was seen in the increase of the number of deep sea ships arriving at New Westminster from 248 in 1929 to 434 in 1935. The three railways serving the docks agreed to give the city port the same import and export rates as Vancouver, making it competitive enough nationally that it could boast that it was the third ranking port in the country. The value of the total tonnage peaked for the decade in 1936 at 1,008,019 tons. The port now saw an increased variety of cargoes being exported, from lead and zinc to apples and grain. The Pacific Coast Terminals was reorganized, with the CPR being a major shareholder along with the Consolidated Mining and Smelter Company. With new investment, the port saw the introduction of mechanical lumber carriers and stackers, cranes, lift trucks and dockside railways.

The big project that really energized the city and forever changed its future was the building of a high-level traffic bridge to replace the old New Westminster Bridge crossing. The city, led by Mayor Hume,

The elaborate May Day celebrations took on an especially festive air when combined with the Silver Jubilee of King George V.

STRIDE STUDIOS PHOTOGRAPH, MAY 3, 1935.
IHP 1090

exerted all its political might in 1933 to quash progress of the low-level Ladner bridge that was in the midst of the planning stage for construction between Delta and Richmond. City council, the Board of Trade and the Harbour Commission jointly cabled a London-based construction company to order it to stop working on the project. They used the opportunity of a provincial election that year to have the question of constructing a high-level bridge in New Westminster put forward and debated in the context of providing better port access.

The leader of the provincial Liberal party, T.D. Pattullo, made the bridge project part of his election platform, and when he won the election he pushed the project forward. The bridge was advocated by Pattullo as part of a public works program to relieve unemployment through both its construction and the economic vitality an improved Pacific Highway would bring. When the four-million-dollar project was introduced to the legislature in 1935, there was widespread dissention over the decision. Vancouver politicians wondered why the little town of New Westminster should be favoured with such an extravagance. With five members of his party opposed, Pattullo was forced to crack the whip to get it approved.

A bright spot in the city's development in the 1930s was the generous community effort to improve its recreational facilities. The Kiwanis Club developed Moody Park's playgrounds and sport facilities and even built this clubhouse, which was opened with a celebration on Eighth Street.

The completed Pattullo Bridge was a glorious achievement and gave New Westminster a towering landmark on the river.

STRIDE STUDIOS PHOTOGRAPH, 1937. IHP 7152

The opening parade for the Pattullo Bridge was led by the New Westminster Regimental Band and a long line of the cars of dignitaries who were not required to pay the hated toll fee on the "Pay-toll-o" bridge.

PHOTOGRAPHER UNKNOWN, NOVEMBER 15, 1937. IHP 8023-01

The province pushed the bridge construction to an early start in October 1935. The size of the bridge and its underwater pier supports, combined with the currents and depth of the river, posed a challenge. This bridge would be an engineering feat. The project renewed the optimism of citizens and had an immediate impact on the landscape of the city, both from the water and on land. The project required the removal of an entire neighbourhood at the bridge head; these historic houses were either moved or demolished. Even the old cenotaph at Leopold Place was relocated, taking up a proud new position at the end of the bridge approach. Opening ceremonies brought thousands into the city on November 15, 1937. Rather than a delicate ribbon cutting, the opening of this massive monument to steel and concrete was celebrated with the premier wielding a welder's torch to cut a chain strung across the road. The bridge was named, with no shame by the government of the day, after the project's champion, Premier Pattullo. Residents hated to face the bridge's toll booths, and soon the crossing was nicknamed the "Pay-Toll-O" Bridge.

After 1935, a renewed enthusiasm for home construction changed the outlying suburban areas of New Westminster completely. The population of the city had increased marginally (by 4,000) during the Depression years, to 22,000 in 1937, but soon accelerated. There was an acute housing shortage and many of the large old homes were being converted into apartments. The city was the first municipality to

Right: *Catching a red-hot flying rivet called for some special tools and nerves of steel.*

H.G. Cox photograph, 1937. (Reprinted from original negative). H.G. Cox collection, courtesy Susan Hopkins.

Below: *The construction of the Pattullo Bridge was one of the largest projects undertaken in the province during the Great Depression.*

Stride Studios photograph, 1936. IHP 1617

negotiate with the B.C. Electric Railway for a change of public transportation from streetcars to more flexible buses to access its growing residential areas. However, the interurban lines continued to operate regionally, with the city as a hub. The switch to buses occurred on December 5, 1938, along with the removal of all of the trolley poles, tracks and wires that had cluttered Columbia Street. The city could now boast a clean modern streetscape that catered only to automobiles. The city's first automatic traffic light signals had also been introduced that year with a ceremony at Sixth Street and Columbia.

The new bus system was inaugurated with a cross-town bus line that connected the growing West End to downtown. The bus line was very popular with locals, and the corner of Eighth Avenue and Twelfth Street became an important junction for shoppers from both directions. Here a new commercial area began to grow, crowned by the $25,000 sleek, modernist-styled Metro Theatre opened by Lieutenant-Governor Hamber in 1938. The need for housing and cheap building lots forced young couples to choose the West End, which was dubbed "Honeymoon Heights." The West End had an estimated population of about 5,000, enough growth to require construction of the new Lord Tweedsmuir School. Even Queensborough, which had languished for years as a farming district, was seeing significant new residential construction and growth, necessitating a larger new Queen Elizabeth School. Local residents grumbled about the city ignoring their needs for sewers and infrastructure. In its splendid isolation, this neighbourhood developed

Above: *The city was one of the first communities in Greater Vancouver to allow the B.C. Electric Railway Company to pull up the tracks of its streetcars and replace them with modern buses. This view of the Eighth Avenue bus line is taken at East Columbia and Braid streets in Sapperton.*

PHOTOGRAPHER UNKNOWN, 1937. IHP 4882

Below: *The Mc & Mc neon clock marked the entrance to the city's commercial district, which began to ride a heady wave of prosperity prior to the Second World War.*

PHOTOGRAPHER UNKNOWN, C. 1940. IHP 3640

Right: *In Queensborough the growing ethnic diversity of New Westminster was wonderfully represented. Here, the Indo-Canadian community poses proudly at the Sikh Temple on Boyne Street at its annual gathering.*

<small>Photographer unknown, September 4, 1932. NWPL 2109</small>

Below: *New Westminster's Italian Mutual Aid Society built its own hall in Queensborough on Ewen Avenue through volunteer labour. This photograph, taken at the opening of the hall, shows the directors of the society and a dance band with three accordions ready to celebrate.*

<small>Photographer unknown, 1932. IHP 8014</small>

a unique community spirit that was made even more remarkable by its cultural diversity.

The city's downtown benefitted from the return to prosperity. It finally saw the construction of some impressive buildings that, with their modern design, evoked the optimism of the era. The old post office received a handsome stone Art Moderne addition in anticipation of the old building's demolition. Another was the new $80,000 warehouse and store of the McLennan, McFeely and Prior Company, popularly known as the "Mc & Mc," located on Columbia between McNeely and Blackie streets. The handsome concrete structure completed in 1939 was hailed as one of the finest and most modern stores in Canada. Designed by Vancouver architects McCarter & Nairne, the building featured a sleek, streamlined Art Moderne exterior and a bright two-storey showroom. Another landmark feature of the building was a huge neon clock sign suspended over the sidewalk.

The end of the Great Depression in New Westminster was signalled with what *The British Columbian* said "will go down in the annals of this historic city as the date of the greatest event in its history."[3] It was announced that, on May 31, 1939, the Royal City would be visited by the King and Queen as part of their Canadian tour. The visit created such a sensation of loyal patriotic fervor that citizens fell into a near state of delirium. Civic officials were told that time constraints allowed no more than a motorcade through the city from Vancouver with a send-off by train. But nothing would dampen the determination of citizens that their city's first true "Royal Visit" would be a success.

The entire route of the royal motorcade was decorated for the event, with every homeowner, business and institution involved in making the route a ceremonial procession. Once completed it was described as

Below, left: *The King and Queen are surrounded by crowds as they leave the gates of Queen's Park. None seemed to mind that the royal couple never bothered to stop en route through the city.*

Below, right: *Mayor Hume greets the King and Queen at the temporary train platform built for their departure at the waterfront on East Columbia Street, in front of the B.C. Penitentiary.*

" … a flame of colour that runs like a river of fire through city streets; these flags, on buildings, on flagpoles, on trees, on anything … are immensely impressive."[4] Twenty-eight elaborate arches of welcome stood over the route, representing every civic group and municipality from the Fraser Valley.

When the royal procession left Kingsway to enter the Royal City they were greeted by a crowd that had swelled the city's population from 22,000 to an estimated 150,000. The roar of cheers from the throngs of people lining the route could be heard throughout the city as the King and Queen made their way to Queen's Park. When they entered the stadium, 11,000 school children gave them a thunderous welcome. As the royal car slowly circled the stadium track 2,700 children were performing on the field in costume, including a display of maypole dancing. On the waterfront a platform had been built in front of the penitentiary, where the official civic party waited. Here the King expressed great surprise at the size of the crowds and, as he shook hands with Mayor Hume, he declared that "New Westminster is a beautiful city." The Queen was presented with flowers by the mayor's daughter, Miss Dorothy Hume. In an unscripted moment, the royal couple crossed the street to greet Mrs. Hume, who had been for years confined to her bed but brought by car for this event. The crowd cheered its approval for this act of kindness. After acknowledging a flotilla of fishing boats and the *Samson* and other craft on the river, they boarded the silver and blue royal train and were taken across the New Westminster Bridge for their return trip across the country.

This royal visit had been a carefully orchestrated prelude to the oncoming war, an effort to ensure that Canada would answer the call of duty everyone knew was coming. When war was declared on September

Below: *The King and Queen wave goodbye to the city as they begin their journey back across Canada on the royal train.*

PHOTOGRAPHER UNKNOWN, MAY 31, 1939. IHP 3624

Below, right: *Columbia Street looked splendid and crowded on the day of the royal visit.*

STRIDE STUDIOS PHOTOGRAPH, MAY 31, 1939. IHP 8013

10, 1939, New Westminster was ready. Unlike the era of the Great War, this new war brought prosperity to the city in the form of progressive industrial growth and expansion.

Immediately the city seemed to buzz with activity and purpose as the war transformed people's lives overnight. Women raided stores to buy everything they could before rationing was imposed. The number of marriages soared as sweethearts were forced to make quick decisions before men sailed overseas. By December the harbour was filled with the grey merchant ships of Great Britain that continued to load cargo in spite of the knowledge of the dangers awaiting them in the Atlantic.

The Westminster Regiment had started training in earnest in 1938 and, with the declaration of war, was mobilized for active service. A military depot was required but all of the parks facilities were considered too important for civic use to turn them over. Instead, the old Douglas Road cemetery at Eighth Street and Tenth Avenue was utilized and

The federal government was getting ready for war and brought the HMCS Fraser *to New Westminster's dock to drum up some patriotism during the May Day celebration.*

tombstones were moved out of the way to accommodate a new barracks facility. Soldiers were stationed and trained here before being issued their marching orders overseas or to another camp for specialized training. The 2nd Battalion of the Westminster Regiment was organized to perform its wartime duties of protecting the homefront with guards stationed at the barracks, the Queen's Park Reservoir, the Armoury, and the Railway Bridge.

The 1st Battalion of the Westminster Regiment immediately filled its ranks with a full strength of 1,000 men for overseas service. The regiment during its operations was said to have "never failed to take an objective and never yield a position to the enemy ... their magnificent combination of courage, skill and leadership resulted in victories often against overwhelming odds and in extremely difficult circumstances." [5] Throughout the war only 3 men were taken prisoner. Their casualties were 467, of which 135 were killed in action or died from their wounds. More than 4,236 officers and men passed through the regiment's ranks.

The most famous photograph taken in New Westminster is this image, popularly known as "Wait for me Daddy." It was taken at the foot of Eighth Street at Columbia and shows the B.C. Regiment DCOR on its way to its war. After its appearance in the Vancouver Province *it was picked by* Life Magazine *as "Picture of the Week" and later chosen as best picture of the year by the press of North America.*

CLAUDE P. DETLOFF PHOTOGRAPHER, OCTOBER 1, 1940. IHP 1956

Above: *New Westminster Victory Loan campaign girls publicized the big War Savings Stamp Dance to be held at the arena in Queen's Park with Dal Richards and the Hotel Vancouver Orchestra.*

STRIDE STUDIOS PHOTOGRAPH, AUGUST 28, 1942. NWPL 3289

Below: *The workers of Seagram Distillery in Sapperton gather to show off their rightfully earned Victory Loan banners.*

STRIDE STUDIOS PHOTOGRAPH, C. 1943. IHP 5790

It had a total time of service of six years and five months. Women too served an important role. In 1939 over 200 city women joined the local detachment of the B.C. Women's Service Club to prepare for local emergencies and support the war effort. Other women left the city to join new women's branches of the military services in addition to serving as nurses.

At home, citizens once again assisted the war effort with impressive results. One of the unique aspects of New Westminster during the war was that it became a temporary home to thousands of men stationed here from across the country undergoing training and awaiting for their transfer to other bases or overseas to the various battlefronts. The Soroptomist Club saw the need to create a "home away from home" for these men to spend their down time in a friendly setting away from the army camp and the bars of Columbia Street. The project, led by Janet Gilley and Dorothea McBride, the sister of the former premier, secured the old Galbraith mansion at Eighth Street and Queens Avenue. It was a city tax sale property earmarked for demolition, but the ladies worked their magic with council and the property was leased for this project.

Mayor Hume officiated at the opening of Westminster House in 1940, which was finely finished and decorated by volunteers with donations from the business community. One soldier wrote of the importance of

Below, top: *Lovely lady volunteers show visiting soldiers a good time at Westminster House.*

PHOTOGRAPHER UNKNOWN, C. 1943. NWPL 2653

Below, bottom: *Crowds gather in front of the Columbia Theatre and Liberty House to see Jack Benny take the stage in a Victory Loan drive.*

PHOTOGRAPHER UNKNOWN, 1943. IHP 7866

this place: "To put into words what Westminster House is doing for the boys in the service is just about as impossible as an Axis victory, and the same applied to how much the boys appreciate their effort … At night you drop in and are practically surrounded by the most lovely girls, who will dance, sing, play cards or just sit and chat with you … for your entertainment … When we leave we will be taking fond memories with us. Instead of just thinking of home we will be thinking of home and Westminster House." [6]

Industry boomed in the city but the port, after some initial activity, had all but shut down. The number of ships visiting port dropped from 511 in 1939 to only 89 in 1943. However, exports by rail grew as both the war industry and Britain needed a continuous supply of B.C. lumber shipped by Atlantic convoy. New industry based on the war effort came to the city in the form of the Canadian Pacific Airplane plant and contracts to Mercer's Star Shipyards, both located in Queensborough. Women donned overalls and turbans to work in the many plants throughout the city. The city's population actually grew during the war to 25,000 by 1944 and once again old houses were renovated into apartments to serve the increased need.

In 1941 the attack on Pearl Harbor brought the war to the Pacific coast and paranoia to British Columbia. Suddenly every town and city with a port felt extremely vulnerable, as the Western Air Command

warned of imminent attack and ordered complete blackouts on December 8, 1941. New Westminster residents read front-page newspaper stories that enemy planes were spotted near San Franscisco. They prepared for Japanese bombs by following the blackout edict. *The British Columbian* reported:

> … the order took many people by surprise and found them unprepared with the result that the black out was a progressive affair. Many were not listening to their radios when the order came … and in most cases the facilities for effectively shrouding windows was not available. City streetlights went out very soon after the order was given but the lights on the Pattullo Bridge remained on after that. The residential districts were at first a checkerboard of light and shade … By this time the A.R.P. wardens were moving about the Stygian gloom of the streets, going to illuminated houses and warning the occupants. Before seven o'clock, there were many cars moving about the darkened street without headlights, the drivers somehow feeling their way … Downtown on Columbia Street the neon signs still blazed. Between seven and eight they were extinguished … driving became extremely hazardous [and there were many accidents]. Across the river the lights went out very slowly but by 10 o'clock, viewed from the highest point of the west end, nothing could be seen but the blinker lights on the river … and away on the hillside in Surrey one lone light shone like a beacon.[7]

Women get to work stacking veneer for the construction of airplanes nicknamed "Mosquitoes" at the Pacific Veneer and Plywood plant. Hanging in the factory are motivational banners reading: "Give us more planes is the pilot's cry—so produce more veneer send them Mosquitoes to fly" and "Birch rolls in … Veneer rolls out … Employees stay home … No Mosquitoes fly out."

LEONARD FRANK PHOTOGRAPH, 1943. IHP 5962

The size of New Westminster's Japanese-Canadian community can be readily imagined from this panoramic photograph taken at the funeral for Mrs. Matzu Nishiguchi held at the Buddhist Temple on Tenth Street.

<small>STRIDE STUDIOS PHOTOGRAPH, FEBRUARY 9, 1936. IHP 8018-002</small>

The large Japanese-Canadian community of the Fraser Valley was immediately faced with a suspicious and hostile population and government. Branded "enemy aliens" in their own country, the passage of orders-in-council under the War Measures Act denied them their basic human rights. The Royal Canadian Navy working with the RCMP began to impound the 1,200 vessels in the Japanese-Canadian fishing fleet, with New Westminster's harbour designated as one of the assembly points. The fishermen were forced to sail their boats into the harbour and turn them over to the government. The boats were moored at the Annieville dike. Many of them sunk over the winter and the remainder were sold in 1942.

In March 1942, the city's entire Japanese-Canadian population was under orders for deportation to interior camps. Initially, they were ordered to surrender their automobiles and obey a curfew of being off the streets by sunset. The community consisted of 288 persons, according to the 1941 census, with 157 children attending city schools at the time. There were about 14 businesses owned by Japanese-Canadians, but the owners, hearing the news, were so shocked they did nothing to try and liquidate their stock. One business owner interviewed by *The British Columbian* said, "I feel like jumping off the Pattullo Bridge ... but for

A soldier of the Westminster Regiment is welcomed home in Queen's Park stadium.

the kids I might do it." [8] In April the first trains taking these families to Alberta and Manitoba to work in the sugar beet fields left from the city's CPR station. These events mark one of the most tragic human-rights violations in the history of Canada.

The news of the end in Europe reached the city on the morning of May 7, 1945. Columbia Street was almost deserted until the arrival of high school students, who left their classes and formed long "snake" parades running through traffic around buses and in and out of the post office. Gradually, the crowd grew and stores hung bunting and flags while office workers threw clouds of shredded paper from windows. From somewhere in the snake line someone started singing and they were soon joined by a band that played "Roll out the Barrel," "Over There," "Hail Hail" and other marching songs.[9] More somber recognition of the war's end came at the impromptu gatherings at the cenotaph and in churches where people observed a moment of silence and reverence for the dead.

Soldiers began to arrive on the Pacific coast in preparation for further battles with Japan until there, too, the war came to a sudden and tragic end. Slowly the city's men and women returned home. The largest celebration of the return of the Westminster Regiment came with the arrival of locomotive #2704 at the old CPR station on the evening of January 19, 1946, to a welcoming crowd of 20,000.

At eight-thirty the bell of the troop train was heard coming from Front Street. Slowly the train edged into view with members of the regiment standing on the steps and crowding the windows. They looked long and hard. They were home. Quickly and smoothly they disembarked from the train and formed up in the street. The crisp bark of CQMS Phil Abbott, Chilliwack, called "on parade" … Efficiency like this carried the Westminster Regiment through some of the toughest fighting on record, to emerge as one of the top fighting units of World War Two. With the command from Lt. Col. Corbould the parade moved off [to Queen's Park] to the tune of "Colonel Bogey" … on the last leg of the long trek that started four years ago. The Westminsters marched into the oval under the moonlight as a faint mist rose from the chilled grass. They tramped to a patch of cold light cast by the floodlights before the platform as, from the dimness of the stands and from the masses who blanketed the corner of the field itself, there rose a roar from 5,000 throats that drowned the trumpets and even the skirl of the … pipe band … relatives had been herded into stands to sit behind family name letters and wait for the ranks to break. While the speeches were being staccatoed off, they swarmed over the field and the khaki ranks were drowned by civvies suits. With laughter and the tears of joy, wives, mothers and fathers and sweethearts were gathering to their arms the warriors who had returned.[10] ✿

Pioneer Filmmaker HUGH NORMAN LIDSTER, 1888–1967

The widespread popularity of photography created many talented amateur photographers; working in obscurity, they left a legacy of extraordinary images. The Royal City owes so much to its honorary "native son" Hugh Norman Lidster, a community leader who loved making motion pictures.

Born in Barrow-in-Furness, Lancashire, England, Hugh Norman Lidster came with his family to British Columbia in 1902 as a lad of 14. He excelled at his early studies but was bored with school. After landing a job in Vancouver as an "office boy" in a legal firm, he found his calling. Lidster was admitted to the bar in 1913 and relocated to New Westminster. His interest in local issues and municipal law led him to politics and he was elected as a councilor in 1925. An appointment to the city's library board soon led to a position on the provincial library board, on which he served for 37 years. In 1946, he was hired as the first city solicitor, a position he retained until his retirement in 1957.

Fascinated by the technology and art of cinematography, Lidster purchased his own movie camera in 1930 and began making home movies. Always an extremely thorough and meticulous individual, he became a member of the Amateur Cinema League (ACL) to hone his filmmaking craft. In 1931 he turned his lens towards the civic May Day celebration, and continued to film this event every year until 1963, amassing a film archive without rival. He also trained his camera on a variety of other events, such as the 1939 royal visit and the celebration of VE day on Columbia Street in 1945.

Lidster was keenly aware of the historic importance of documentation and preservation. He was one of the city staff given the task of organizing the purchase of Irving House in 1950 and served proudly on its board until 1958. He would no doubt be pleased to learn of the preservation of his incredible photographic legacy. His son Wallace cared for the collection of over 75 film canisters from Lidster's death until 1997. Wallace then brought three dusty boxes to the home of his sister, Freda Springate, and she enlisted her son Nick to take on the task of transferring the film to digital media. The results were outstanding: flicker-free broadcast-quality images. The family donated the historically valuable Hugh Norman Lidster collection to the New Westminster Museum and Archives in 2005. •

Top: Self-portrait. HUGH N. LIDSTER FILM STILL, C. 1930. **Above:** High school students celebrate VE day with a snake parade on Columbia Street. HUGH N. LIDSTER FILM STILL. COURTESY NICK SPRINGATE.

CHAPTER 8

The Golden Mile 1945–1960

Previous page: *Columbia Street is enjoying its status as the "Golden Mile" in this winter scene of 1948. The record snowfall would be a contributing factor to the flood later that year.*

Immediately following the war, New Westminster was humming along with all the vitality and pace of the era's big band music. Economic prosperity and progress were present in every industry and corner of the city. The city's industrial base grew as the demand for British Columbia's resources in the post-war world economy expanded at a phenomenal rate.

This boom brought people to the Lower Mainland, both from across Canada and from war-torn Europe. New subdivisions such as Victory Heights, named to honour the men and women who won the war, finally took up some of the remaining vacant land in the city. However, New Westminster's actual rate of growth was modest in comparison to the other larger suburban municipalities outside Vancouver. The population of the city grew from an estimated 25,000 in 1945 to an official census count of 33,654 in 1961. In 1951 the city saw only a 31 percent increase in its population while the rest of suburban Greater Vancouver saw its population grow by 43 percent. Within its small boundaries, the Royal City was quickly running out of the vacant land that had allowed its longstanding pattern of expansion through single-family residential development.

Although its population growth was stagnating, the city's role as an industrial hub was taking on greater importance; it could boast that it was second only to Vancouver as a great centre of trade and manufacturing. In 1946 its total construction boom of four million dollars was largely attributed to the expansion of such industrial plants as Westminster Ironworks and Heaps Limited. By 1947 even the harbour shipping totals had returned to pre-war levels, and by the 1950s, record tonnages were recorded. *The Vancouver Sun* declared that the Royal City "commercially and industrially ... reaps all the benefits of a city five times the population."[1] Of course, while the city's industrial plants created employment for many of the residents in surrounding suburbs, the city also raked in the taxes from these industries to feed its own services.

This boom was especially evident in the city's lumber industries, with lumber exports growing 150 percent. Six thousand of the city's 8,500 industrial workers were employed by the lumber manufacturing sector. Knowing their importance, workers affiliated with the International

Woodworkers union staged a bitter month-long strike in 1946 to hold onto wartime gains and establish a 40-hour work week. The strike sent shivers through the local economy, as an estimated 85 cents of every dollar spent in the city's shops came from the wages provided by the lumber industry. But this strike was one of the few of the era, as workers and management were pleased to ride the waves of prosperity that were transforming the city and society.

Anticipating post-war growth and fearing urban chaos, New Westminster city council followed the lead of Vancouver and hired the famous American town planner Harland Bartholomew to create a plan for the modern city. A series of influential and comprehensive plans for zoning, parks, schools, transportation and a civic centre were produced between 1945 and 1947. Although the city had adopted an official zoning bylaw in 1940, the development of the modern city did not come until after the war. The need and trend for new civic buildings was formulated by the Bartholomew plan, which advocated relocating city hall and creating a civic centre.

The Bartholomew plan also entrenched the vision for the rapid transition of this suburban city into a more urban place through designating higher-density apartment developments at the eastern end of the downtown area, below Royal Avenue. The residential areas to the

A panorama of the construction of post-war "Victory Homes" on Nanaimo Street east of Twelfth Street.

west of Sixth Street and in Sapperton between Richmond and Columbia streets became new two-family districts as a transition to their future conversion into apartment areas. The post-war housing crisis fueled the continued conversion of many of the city's old homes into apartments.

Bartholomew created a 1946 plan for the school board to replace old facilities with new junior and senior high schools on the old city works yard site and former military camp on Eighth Street. Financial difficulties forced the school board to proceed with the junior high school first in order to relieve the overcrowding of both elementary and senior secondary facilities. The provincial government provided the necessary joint funding to proceed and plans for the school were completed in 1947. Construction of the 1.5-million-dollar project began the following year. The old buildings on the site were plowed away along with the few remaining visible vestiges of the old Douglas Road cemetery, which had served as the city's pioneer cemetery before becoming a potter's field. The many graves remained in place, although one bulldozer did manage to unearth a coffin, creating lurid headlines.

On December 16, 1949, the New Westminster Junior High School was opened with a full ceremony presided over by British Columbia's premier, Byron I. Johnson. W.T. Straith, Minister of Education, praised the city for its intention of utilizing the new school for adult educa-

Swanky suburban bungalows of the new Massey Heights area made the Royal City proud. Note the TV antennas on every roof in this view of the 800 block of Massey Street.

CROTON STUDIOS, C. 1955. IHP 1819

tion through night schools and cultural activities in the auditorium and gymnasium. It was the lavish auditorium or theatre that received high praise from civic officials, who claimed it was the finest in the Pacific Northwest. The facility was recognized as forming the beginning of what was hoped to be a new civic centre for New Westminster. The junior high school was later named after Governor General Vincent Massey, a name that lives on to this day in the Massey Theatre. The school was one of the largest and finest examples of early Modern institutional structures in the city. Its original design featured a rough cast stucco exterior with round windows and vents, tall theatrical bay entrance, sleek bands of wood windows, flagpole and signage, altogether creating a distinctive modernist architectural landmark.

The prosperity following the war was severely tested by the greatest disaster to ever hit the Fraser Valley; the flood of May–June 1948. A heavy mountain snow pack, combined with a late spring and a sudden snap of hot weather, sent water levels near to the heights of the record 1894 flood. The destruction began in the province's interior as melting snow filled every creek and river. A 15-foot "wall of water" tore through dikes and inundated the low-lying farms and villages of the upper Fraser Valley. Buildings and homes were under water, some being picked up from their foundations and carried away. Soon the entire valley was in

Below, top: *The junior high school had many modern features, including a home economics classroom where young women could learn to be perfect homemakers.*

B.C. MINISTRY OF EDUCATION PHOTOGRAPH, 1950. IHP 8015-02

Below, bottom: *The new junior high school on Eighth Avenue looked like a pretty cool place for the city's teenagers to hang out.*

B.C. MINISTRY OF EDUCATION PHOTOGRAPH, 1950. IHP 8015-01

turmoil, with 16,000 people evacuated from their homes. The roads and railways connecting the valley to the rest of the province were under water or destroyed in sections. A state of emergency was declared and the frigate HMCS *Antigonish* arrived at New Westminster to serve as an emergency aid headquarters to launch naval boats upriver to rescue the hundreds of people stranded on roofs.

The city experienced minor flooding that threatened the main business district as water rose during record high tides to cover the docks and lap at the back door of the B.C. Electric Railway station on Front Street. The foot of Twelfth Street was also under water but did not cause panic or serious damage. The situation in Queensborough, however, with 5,000 residents living on the floodplain in the direct path of the Fraser's fury, was dire, as it was protected only by ancient dikes that had been long neglected.

When waters started rising it was Scotty McKenzie, a 73-year-old riverfront squatter with a wooden leg, who took action. He had lived on the Mississippi during the flood of 1926 and had great experience building and maintaining dikes. "It became known that an elderly man with one leg was working night and day patching soggy dikes. 'Scotty' was seen to wade waist-deep in cold water to lay a key bag properly and to kick his wooden leg into rat holes which threatened to undermine structures ... His knowledge was accepted and his word became law which was backed up by Mayor W.M. Mott as well as by military authorities. He became in a sense, a field marshal but continued to work with a fervor that served as an inspiration to others." [2]

The frigate HMCS Antigonish *was an impressive sight at the city dock during the flood.*

A few members of the naval crew of the HMCS Antigonish *are seen enjoying a break from their duties.*

Bases of weakened dikes were bolstered with sandbags and gravel and height was added until they were five to seven sandbags above the normal level. Thousands of civilian volunteers rallied to the emergency, made more ominous by the curtailing of all sporting events in New Westminster. The Westminster Regiment came back into force, with over 300 troops on the scene under the direction of commanding officer Lieutenant Colonel F.C.B. Cummins. Hundreds of military and civilian vehicles were put into action hauling men and material to the dikes. The operation cost over $26,000, of which $10,000 was spent on acquiring the estimated one million sandbags.

As the danger of the flood heightened on June 7, Colonel Cummins and Mayor Mott ordered the voluntary evacuation of Queensborough. Families determined to save their homes and businesses refused to leave, much to the consternation of authorities. The Red Cross headquarters aided over 300, mainly women and children, who took refuge from the flood threat. It was feared that, if the dike broke, a wall of water would tear across the flat terrain of Queensborough and literally drown its residents. The only escape would be Ewen Avenue and the bridge to the city. A railway engine was stationed on the tracks with 20 flat cars and boxcars ready to carry everyone out should the dikes not hold.

During the height of the crisis, with water rising everywhere, the main Queensborough pump became plugged with debris. The city's chief engineer, R.E. Potter, took charge and dove into the cold slimy water. After nine dives, he cleared the pump. On June 10, with the peak tide, the Fraser River rose an incredible 14 feet, 4 inches. Volunteers stood precariously on the dikes to keep a careful watch on their handiwork. After the bolstered levees stood the test, everyone heaved a huge collective sigh of relief. Queensborough had been saved thanks to the massive community effort.

During this era New Westminster's downtown was experiencing a complete renaissance as the centre of commerce and business for the entire region. Columbia Street especially seemed to embody the spirit of the new era. The streets were alive and customers filled the stores, restaurants and bars. Long-time businesses were achieving record profits and Columbia Street was celebrated as having the highest sales per square foot in the entire province. With this prosperity, long-established stores expanded and modernized and many other companies moved in, hoping to cash in on what was termed the "Golden Mile."

The city too cashed in on the success of the street in 1947 by taking the advice of Harland Bartholomew and moving the City Market to the west end of Columbia Street to stimulate the renewal of the western part of the city. With thousands of customers daily, the City Market was expected to finally rejuvenate the former district of Chinatown. With funds from the sale of the former site, a new $110,000 modern market building of concrete and steel, with over 26,000 square feet of space, was designed by talented architect Percy Underwood. Once again the market's significance to the Fraser Valley was recognized, this time by the attendance at the opening on August 22, 1947, of Frank Putnam, the provincial Minister of Agriculture. Great progress for the area was predicted at the opening ceremonies, but history would prove otherwise.

The old market building and historic Lytton Square were sold to David Spencer Ltd., which would be absorbed by the T. Eaton and Company B.C. Ltd. Eaton and Company was proud to open "a new modern and impressive store."[3] The building, designed by C.B.K. Van Norman in modern style, was in reality a massive renovation that had amalgamated three historic buildings. By adding another storey to the old City Market and putting on a modernist face, the new renovation all but obliterated the historic City Market and Liberty Block facing Columbia Street. On the Front Street side, however, the form of the old buildings, especially the Lytton Hotel, can still be discerned.

The building was a boost to the confidence of the Royal City in the heady post-war years. Officially opened by Mayor Sangster and other dignitaries in 1949, the building was finished in white, with gleaming stainless steel showcase windows, "majestic" glass doors and black marble, making it one of the most imposing and stylish stores on Columbia Street. Every possible convenience for the shopper was considered; Eaton's was particularly proud of its new Motorstair, the first escalator in the Fraser Valley, carrying customers with ease up to the various levels of the store.

The city's Native Sons and Daughters were not forgotten in the rush to demolish every historic building in the quest for a modern city. The Native Daughters' long-held dream to preserve the historic 1865 residence of Captain William and Elizabeth Irving finally became a reality in

The Native Sons and Daughters knew how to make history fun, setting aside historical accuracy to sport Wild West costumes to ride the famous Dufferin Coach and promote the opening of Irving House Historic Centre.

ON-THE-SPOT-PHOTOGRAPHERS, 1950. IHP 1145

Above, top: *The Eaton's department store was one of the key anchor merchants of the "Golden Mile."*

DOMINION PHOTO COMPANY, 1949. NWPL 1515

Above, bottom: *The new B.C. Electric bus depot at Sixth Street and Royal Avenue was an impressive and modern addition to the city.*

WALKER & WARD SCENIC POSTCARD, 1953. AUTHOR'S COLLECTION

Right: *Staff members of the city's engineering department are seen in their second-floor office of the old city hall, planning for the post-war boom.*

PHOTOGRAPHER UNKNOWN, C.1952. IHP 7411

1950. Mayor J. Lewis Sangster personally brokered the deal to secure the house from the Irving's granddaughters, Naomi and Manuella Briggs. The deal was sealed when the mayor told city council that if operating the museum proved too expensive then the site would make an impressive profit as an apartment site. At the opening ceremony Mayor Sangster paid tribute to his fellow council members for their support and handed over a golden key to the Native Daughters. In his speech he explained that the new historic centre was " ... more than just a building—It is the City! and the place for the things that are precious to us."[4] Finally a permanent home for historic treasures was accomplished, and one of the truly great historic collections of British Columbia began to take shape with valued donations from pioneer families of the city.

With the new suburban boom came a complete transformation of transportation in the Lower Mainland. In the 1950s, the B.C. Electric Railway Company quickly moved to modernize the company with buses and put its old interurban depot on Columbia Street up for sale. It purchased a portion of the now-closed Howay School site on Royal Avenue and Sixth Street from the city for a new swanky modern-styled administration building and bus depot, opened on June 10, 1952. New Westminster's hub locations for interurban railways finally came to a close in 1953 with the abandonment of the rail services to Vancouver.

The City of New Westminster also decided to make the move to uptown by taking over the soon-to-be-closed Duke of Connaught High School site across the street to build an impressive city hall. Using funds from the sale of both the Howay School and old city hall sites, combined with a ratepayer-approved bylaw, a budget of $600,000 gave city council the funds to create a truly splendid building. Described as "palatial," the new hall featured some beautiful modern interior designs accomplished

by architect A.C. Smith. The council chamber was lined with "oyster walnut" panelling and councilors could now sit rather regally at walnut desks. The cenotaph was moved from its less-than-ideal location at the Pattullo Bridge to take up a more fitting and ceremonial location amid a garden landscape on the building's great lawn. Mayor Fred Jackson declared the building open on November 19, 1953, dedicating it for the "perpetuation of good government." [5]

The removal of transportation and civic facilities foreshadowed a significant shift in the city's development. All of the boom factors that had contributed to the glowing rise of Columbia Street as the "Golden Mile" soon led to its demise. Shopping centres were beginning to locate on major highways, closer and more accessible to the suburban homes of their customers. Booming Burnaby saw the Simpsons-Sears Department Store open at Nelson and Kingsway, with acres of free parking. Soon Coquitlam, Surrey and other communities too were blessed with shopping malls—the icons of suburbia.

From within the Royal City, the threat to downtown came in the form of a new Woodward's Department Store. Instead of choosing the congested and expensive Columbia Street, "Chunky" Woodward bought out almost a block of small stores and houses at Sixth Avenue and Sixth Street. This had been a quiet place first occupied by a small corner store built by C.P. Bussey in 1923. Everyone in town thought he was all wet for building a store way out in the bushes away from downtown, but envied the profit he realized from selling out to Woodward's. The sod was turned in 1952 for the four-million-dollar project that transformed uptown New Westminster into the new centre of the city. Soon afterward, others rushed in to buy lots and invest by building new offices and shops, including the Bank of Montreal and the B.C. Telephone Company.

The new city hall fulfilled every citizen's expectations of it to convey the importance of New Westminster.

When Woodward's opened at 10 o'clock on March 11, 1954, crowds had been lined up since 8:30. Customers came from as far away as Chilliwack for the day, and by the time the ribbon was cut, there were four thousand people waiting to get into the store. The Vancouver *Province* reported that " ... it was like the opening of the first city market more than 60 years ago."[6] Thousands came to inspect the colourful, sprawling building declared as Canada's most modern corner store. The newspaper predicted that the heart of the two-storey building would be the grocery department; covering an area of 30,000 square feet, it was New Westminster's largest food market. The reporter then went on to rhapsodize over the magic-eye doors, the 125-foot vegetable counter and the 100-foot self-service meat counter, the 50-foot frozen food display case. The most popular of several innovations, and the stake in the heart of downtown business owners, was the free rooftop parking for 300 family cars, while three auxiliary adjacent lots would have space for 450 more.

Citizens loved the convenience of the city's new uptown, away from the "heart-stopping hill," with easy access either by car or by foot. Columbia Street seemed to have acquired an unwholesome air about it, with all the hotel beer parlours filled with longshoremen and lumber workers. Perhaps mothers felt more comfortable strolling with their children on the clean, wide, uncluttered streets amidst modern buildings. Council also agreed that this location was much preferred and soon purchased a site at Sixth Avenue and Ash Street to build a new library to replace the old Carnegie Library. A modern building was constructed, once again setting the standard for civic pride. It was opened in 1958 by Canada's Governor General, Vincent Massey.

The opening of Woodward's and the success of uptown set off an instant and distinct panic among the downtown merchants. They saw their precious dreams of the Golden Mile slipping away practically

Below, top: *The curious along with opening-day bargain seekers flood into Woodward's shortly after the ribbon-cutting ceremony.*

BOB DIBBLE PHOTOGRAPH, MARCH 11, 1954.
IHP 8021-3

Below, bottom: *A crowd estimated at 4,000 filled the intersection of Sixth Avenue and Sixth Street for the opening of Woodward's.*

BOB DIBBLE PHOTOGRAPH, MARCH 11, 1954.
IHP 8021-1

overnight as shoppers abandoned the old street for sleek modern shopping centres. Meetings were held and, in 1954, the New Westminster Downtown Business and Property Owners Association was formed with 50 members. Membership concluded that the downtown shopping district could compete with the shopping malls only by becoming like them. The first problem to tackle was the lack of parking. Even the new City Market was struggling to achieve customers in the new economy. After much lobbying of council and residents, the solution of erecting a parking ramp structure over top of Front Street was passed by bylaw in 1957. Its speedy construction had the new "Parkade" open for business in February 1959. However, in many ways it was a futile effort; the "Golden Mile" era for Columbia Street was over.

Downtown New Westminster could still attract sizable crowds, despite the competition. It was, after all, still the financial and government centre for much of the Fraser Valley. In 1955 the federal government had enough faith in the area to purchase the old city hall site and undertake the long-awaited expansion of their post office, customs and other government offices that had started in 1939. Unfortunately, the project included the demolition of the beautiful old hall and post office. The new million-dollar building designed by the federal Department of Public Works

May Day celebrations during this era achieved a remarkable makeover into a huge local celebration with elaborate displays of costumes and schoolchildren performing on the fields of Queen's Park.

Photographer unknown, May 10, 1952.
IHP 1507

Right: *Downtown was a marvellous hub of activity, as can be seen in this view of Columbia Street looking east from Eighth Street.*

Frank Goodship photograph, 1955. IHP 8022-001

Below: *New Westminster's waterfront at the foot of Eighth Street retained its charm at the old government docks, home to many visiting fishboats. In the background is the building later converted into the famous King Neptune seafood restaurant.*

Industrial Photographics photograph, c. 1955. IHP 7156

Above: *The new Queensborough Bridge provided an impressive new access to the sparsely settled Lulu Island and the new industrial park of Delta's Annacis Island.*

CROTON STUDIO, C.1960. NWPL 455

Right: *The new St. Mary's Hospital was a much-loved institution in which many new residents were born.*

DOMINION PHOTO COMPANY PHOTOGRAPH, 1959. NWPL 1530

was very modern, reflecting a rather "Stalinist" type of architecture that seemed appropriate only to big government. Nevertheless, the building thrilled local merchants desperate for signs of progress and was appreciated widely by citizens upon its completion in 1959.

On the eve of its centennial in 1960, New Westminster was truly riding a wave of prosperity. The entire city was feeling the effects of tremendous growth and opportunity. The completion of the Massey Heights subdivision on the contoured edge of Victory Heights brought the clean lines of the suburban dream to the city, along with the construction of two stylish shopping centres at Eighth Avenue and McBride Boulevard. St. Mary's Hospital received provincial government approval to raze the inadequate old building and construct a new 150-bed hospital. New apartments and commercial developments across the city were changing the skyline and finally pushing the population figures higher and out of stagnation. Even Queensborough was entering a new era as it prepared to celebrate the opening of its new bridge over the Fraser River.

The fast-paced development of the city did have its critics. City planner Mary Rawson issued a warning during the centennial year:

> The Royal City is the "Sleeping Beauty" of the Lower Mainland. And it's in for a rude awakening … The early citizens of New Westminster made tremendous strides and built the Royal City into the capital city of the Lower Mainland today. But we are in danger of losing this position if we don't stop considering it our birthright and revive civic interest … We need the foresight of the early citizens who built the first school, sailed the first ferry across the Fraser River and established the city's electrical distribution system. This is what has brought us to an historical position of a governmental, financial and business centre … We cannot jog along in our well-worn rut … Our increasing population is being packed away in lunch-box apartments

The Tragedy of Stride Studios CHARLES EDGAR STRIDE, 1890–1972

Charlie Stride was born in New Westminster, the son of Eber and Mary Stride, who pioneered a home and nursery business in Burnaby's Edmonds district. As a young man he too worked in the family business and later tried his hand at building houses. In 1915 he gave it all up for adventure and bought a bicycle to travel to the World's Fair in San Francisco. He liked the trip so much he kept peddling all the way to Tijuana, Mexico. Upon his return to New Westminster he enlisted to fight in the war and was no sooner in England when the armistice was declared.

He returned home and, in 1920, decided to be a photographer. With no training or experience he borrowed a camera from his friend Arthur Insley and, with $100 in capital, began taking "snaps" and developing them. In 1922 he purchased a brass and wood Eastman camera for $500 to begin taking portraits, and in 1925 he opened Stride Studios and boldly challenged six other local firms for business. Charlie was quite a shrewd businessman and secretly purchased the Columbia Studios, located across the street from his business. Whenever he was faced with a disgruntled customer he told them they could take their business elsewhere and pointed them in the direction of Columbia Studios. For 30 years no one knew that he owned the competition.

Stride soon acquired an automatic self-focusing enlarger and high-gloss dryer, becoming one of the best-equipped commercial photography studios in B.C. With a staff of 10, Stride Studios grew to occupy the entire upper floor of 657 Columbia Street. The firm was able to secure contracts as the official photographer for the police departments of the province and surrounding municipalities, the New Westminster Board of Trade, the Harbour Commission, the May Day Committee, the Royal Agricultural and Industrial Society, the Royal Columbian Hospital and the school board, to name a few.

By the 1960s Stride Studios had become even more legendary and historic than many of its photographic subjects. A confirmed batchelor, Stride was proud of the fact that he had no wife who would throw anything out. In his large, rambling studio, Stride had amassed a carefully indexed collection of every single one of his negatives. These 60,000 images included over 10,000 outdoor pictures documenting every significant civic event and over 50,000 portraits of the city's citizens.

On Sunday, December 22, 1968, at 2:30 p.m., Charlie Stride awoke from a nap in his apartment at the back of the studio to see flames leaping out of the window of the building next door. He rushed to telephone the fire department, shocked to realize that his beloved studio and collection was jeopardized by a small fire that had grown to take over two commercial business blocks. When fire crews arrived they poured so much water into the studio that negatives and prints floated out of the building and into the gutters of Columbia Street. Firemen did their best to rescue what they could, but the blaze had destroyed one of the city's most valuable photographic collections. Stride put on a brave face after the fire, but he was deeply wounded by the loss. He died in 1972 and was mourned by many. •

Top: STRIDE STUDIOS PHOTOGRAPH, C. 1950. IHP 1984. **Bottom:** Charlie Stride balances on the top of a stepladder with his camera trained on Columbia Street to capture yet another historic New Westminster scene. PHOTOGRAPHER UNKNOWN, C. 1940. IHP 4748.

built chock-a-block along streets choked with parked cars. Our trees and park lands are disappearing and no public effort is being made to save them. Blight and decay will spread if our appetite for the fast buck eats away our publicly-owned land. We must develop an action program of planning and improvement on all fronts or we are in danger of losing our historic position by default.[7]

Newspaper columnist Barry Mather was more traditionally optimistic about the city's future:

By any standard New Westminster is a Royal City. Her past, her present and the prospect of her future, her location, resources and commerce all make her distinguished in Canada. Third city of B.C. in population New Westminster is second industrially. She ranks fifth in Canada in terms of export tonnage and her port is of world significance. The annual gross value of her manufactured products approaches the $100 million mark ... She is a lumber milling hub, she is the base of the Fraser River fishing fleet, she is a merchandising centre for the lower Fraser Valley, she is the home of more than 100 industries and she is the leading fresh water port of the Pacific. Few cities can look back over a century more remarkable.[8]

An aerial view of downtown New Westminster shows the new parkade that was built in an effort to stem the exodus of shoppers to suburban shopping malls.

CROTON STUDIOS PHOTOGRAPH, 1959. IHP 8016

Above: *New Westminster celebrates its centennial with a huge May Day parade down Columbia Street.*

<small>Bob Dibble photograph, 1960. ihp 8021</small>

Below: *On a wet December evening Columbia Street's "Golden Mile" glows with crowds of shoppers strolling by brightly lit store windows, neon signs and holiday decorations.*

<small>Photographer unknown, c.1960s. nwpl 1705</small>

These two visions of the city in the year of 1960 provide such a point of contrast. Certainly the city in its centennial year embraced both truths. The future ahead would be bright, but filled with challenges. In so many ways, downtown New Westminster appears to have never recovered from losing the "Golden Mile" that existed ever so briefly for Columbia Street. Progress and the ever-increasing growth and change of the cityscape have continued unabated. The industrial city, once so proudly boasted of, now appears so vastly diminished as to be a mere point of history. There have been important losses of civic amenities, green space and trees because of "fast buck" development in the name of the "lunch-box apartment." Century-old institutions and their landmarks, such as the much loved St. Mary's Hospital, can be simply demolished, leaving nothing behind but memories and history. But despite these regrettable losses there have also been tremendous improvements and progress that make New Westminster a remarkable place to live.

The city's centennial of 1960 was marked rather simply by the construction of Centennial Lodge in Queen's Park, with its hall and nearby bandstand and picnic grounds. It remains a place for people to come together and enjoy being part of this city. The building is even occupied by the Arts Council and the venerable Queen's Park Preschool, where children begin to learn the true meaning of community. If there was one true legacy of the first one hundred years, it is that New Westminster's history forged a unique identity and pride of place. It is seen in the steadfast traditions of May Day, the Ancient and Honourable Hyack Anvil Battery's Victoria Day anvil salute and even the more recent Heritage Preservation Society's annual heritage homes tour. These events are now all part of our Hyack Festival, a celebration reminiscent of the great exhibitions of years ago. This incredibly tangible and vibrant sense of community spirit and pride lives on in spite of constant change, leaving a legacy for all of us to celebrate. ✵

This list of New Westminster's photographers and their studios is based in part on the comprehensive Camera Workers' website of David Mattison and used with his kind permission. The list represents only those photographers who operated a known commercial or artistic studio in the city. Mattison's work has been augmented with further detailed directory searches and references found in local newspapers. As directories are notorious for their inaccuracy and omissions, this list is by no means complete. Researchers should also refer to the Camera Workers' website for additional sources and information.

Camera Workers: The British Columbia, Alaska and Yukon Photographic Directory:
http://members.shaw.ca/bchistorian/cw1858–1950.html

Atkinson, J.B.
1889: Columbia Street

B.C. Photo & Fine Art Studio
1892–1895: 441 Columbia Street
(Wintemute Block)
Operated by S.J. Thompson.

Bovill, Wheatley and William Bovill
(Bovill Brothers, *Thompson and Bovill*)
1886: Columbia Street (opposite Colonial Hotel)
1890: Columbia Street (Wintemute Block)

Brighton Studio
1924–1925: 657 Columbia Street
(Armstrong-Curtis Block)
Operated by C.E. Stride.

Browne, John Lothian
(Browne's Photo Studio, Sun Beam Photo Studio)
1884: Columbia Street (over Leiser's store)
1891–1894: 435 Columbia Street
(Wintemute Block)
1892–1898: 437 Columbia/24 Sixth Street
(Ellard Block)

Burlin, Frederick Mauritz
(b.1915–d.1995)
(Burlin's Studio, Burlin Studios)
1948–1977: 515 Sixth Street

Campbell Studio
1928: 35 Sixth Street
Operated by F.E. Colter.

Clowes Studio of Photography
1951–1960: 512 Sixth Avenue
Operated by Don C. Clowes.

Colter, F.E.
See Campbell Studio.

Columbia Studio.
1928–1960: 624 Columbia Street
(Hamley Block)
Managed by C.H. Reeves, 1928–1959, and by Mrs. M. Christensen in 1960, but owned anonymously by C.E. Stride.

Cooksley, William Thomas
(b.1856–d.1913)
1901–1913: 432 Eighth Street
(Private Residence)

Cornish, John Charles
(b.1856–d.1935)
1901–1906: 229 Columbia Street
(Curtis-Armstrong Block)

Cox, Horace Gordon
(b.1885–d.1972)
1924–1955: River Road/2011 Sixth Avenue
(Private Residence)

Croton Studio
(Croton Photo Service)
1949–1960: 911 Twelfth Street
[1961–1978: 7155 Kingsway, Burnaby]
Operated by R.M. LeBlanc and D.F. LeBlanc.

Davis, W.T.
See On-the-Spot Photographers.

Dibble, Robert
See Croton Studios.

Easthope, Frederick E.
(b.1875–d.1967)
(Easthope Studio, Easthope & Co.)
1894–1904: 624 Columbia Street
(Hamley Block)

Fox, Miss E.M.
1919–1920: #513–709 Columbia Street
(Westminster Trust Block)

Fulton, Christopher
1862–1864: Columbia Street
(Columbia Hotel)

Garraway, Lionel Rudolph Henry
(b.1890–d.1936)
1920–1924

Hacking, Frederick Louis
1905–1910: 266 Columbia Street
(Hamley Block)

Haweis, Lionel Thomas Joy
(b.1870–d.1942)
(Royal Studio)
1908: 286 Columbia Street
(Cunningham Block)
Heckley, Albert
1891: Columbia Street (Caledonia Hotel)

Heckley, Joseph Woodward
(Mountain & Heckley)
1891–1895: 437 Columbia Street
(Wintemute Block)

Heslop, Mrs.
1886: Front Street (opposite C.P.N. Co. wharf)

Home Portrait Studio
1914: 440 E. Columbia Street (Sapperton)
Operated by Mrs. Agnes Wiggin.

Hughes, F.B.
See On-the-Spot Photographers.

Hurndall, Frank Ivan Atkinson
(b.1894–d.1978)
(F. Hurndall & Co.)
1918–1921: 614 Columbia Street
1922–1923: 40 Sixth Street
1924–1928: 628 Columbia Street*
Listed as dealer in photographic supplies only.

Judkins, David Roby
(b.1836–d.1909)
(Judkins Floating Sunbeam Gallery)
1882: This floating barge studio visited the city and was tied up to the city dock.

Leash, Homer Ellsworth
1911–12: Photographer for W.J. Kerr Ltd., a real estate and insurance firm.
1913: Photographer with Schwenk's Studio.
1914–1916: 657 Columbia Street
(Armstrong-Curtis Block)

Le Blanc, Don
See Croton Studios.

Le Blanc, R.M.
See Croton Studios.

McDermaid, Albert
1890: Agnes Street

Mathers, Charles W.
(Mather's Studio)
1918–1919: 657 Columbia Street
(Armstrong-Curtis Block)

Matthews, Charles H.
See Rexall Photo Studio.

Mavius, Harold
(b.1867–d.1911)
(Royal Studio)
1909–1911: 610 Columbia Street
(Cunningham Block)

May, Mrs. F.A.
(Royal Studio)
1905–1908: 610 Columbia Street
(Cunningham Block)

Mountain, Albert
(Uren and Mountain, Mountain and
Heckley)
1889–1891: 437 Columbia Street
(Wintemute Block)

Mountain and Heckley
1891: 437 Columbia Street
(Wintemute Block)
See A. Mountain and J.W. Heckley.

Murchie, Archibald
(b.1852–d.1930)
1890–1895: 1411 Sixth Ave.
(Private Residence)

Okamura, Paul L. (Tsunenojo)
(b.1865–d.1937)
c.1895–1902: Blackwood Street
(St. Louis College)
1902–1914: 91 or 99 Fourth Street
(Private Residence)
1914–1930: 719 Carnarvon Street
(Carnarvon Block)
1931–1937: 405 Royal Avenue
(Private Residence)

On-the-Spot Photographers
1946–1952: 520 Sixth Avenue
1953–1955: 2124 London Street
(Private Residence)
Operated by W.T. Davis and F.B. Hughes.

Patterson, M.
1894: Columbia Street (Begbie Block)

Paull, Alfred Albert
(b.1871–d.1958)
1903

Raymond Studios
1955: 753 Carnarvon Street

Reeves, Cecil Heppenstall
(b.1884–d.1969)
See Columbia Studio.

Rexall Photo Studio
1919–1922: 657 Columbia Street
(Armstrong-Curtis Block)
*Owned and managed by C.H. Matthews
from 1919–1921 and by John Vanderpant
in 1922.*

Ritchie, Samuel J.
(b.1863–d.1933)
1909–1914: 657 Columbia Street
(Armstrong-Curtis Block)

Royal Studio
1905–1914: 610 Columbia Street
(Cunningham Block)
*Owned and managed by Mrs. F.A. May,
1905–1908; L.T.J. Haweis, 1908;
Harold Mavius, 1909–1911; and
Mrs. Agnes Wiggins, 1911–1914.*

Russell, Vincent Calhoun
(Russell's Photo Studio)
1918–1921: 625 Columbia Street
(Smith Block)

Schwenk, John Leon
(Schwenk's Studio)
1911–1914: 624 Columbia Street
(Hamley Block)

Steffens-Colmer Studio Ltd.
1930: 552 Columbia Street (Ellis Block)

Stride, Charles Edgar
(b.1890–d.1972)
(Universal Photographers, 1918–1925;
Brighton Studio, 1924–1925; and
Stride Studios, 1926–1968)
1918–1968: 657 Columbia Street
(Armstrong-Curtis Block)
See also Columbia Studio.

Sunbeam Photo Studio
See J.L. Browne.

Thompson, Stephen Joseph
(b.1864–d.1929)
(Thompson and Bovill,
Thompson's Studio)
1886–1888: Columbia Street
(opposite Colonial Hotelº
1888–1898: 620 Columbia Street
(Hamley Block)
c. 1899: 411 Columbian Street
(Burr Block)
1901–1905: 624 Columbia
(Hamley Block)

Thompson & Bovill
1886–1888: Columbia Street
(opposite Colonial Hotel)
See S.J. Thompson and William Bovill.

Universal Photographers
1918–1925: 657 Columbia Street
(Armstrong-Curtis Block)
See C.E. Stride.

Uren, John Batrel
(b.1841–d.1919)
(Uren and Mountain)
1879–1881: McKenzie Street
1882–1883: Front Street
1884–1889: Columbia Street

Uren & Mountain
1889: Columbia Street, near
Church Street
See J.B. Uren and A. Mountain.

Vanderpant, John
(b.1884–d.1939)
(Vanderpant Photo Studio and
Vanderpant Galleries)
1920–1924: 657 Columbia Street
(Curtis Block)
1925–1926: 624 Columbia Street
(Hamley Block)
See Rexall Photo Studio.

Welsh, Howard M.
(b.1869–d.1938)
(Welsh and Company)
1892–1898: 437 Columbia Street
(Wintemute Block)
1899–1903: 229 Columbia Street
(Armstrong-Curtis Block)

Wescott, Stanley Haughton
(b.1896–d.1967)
1922: 625 Columbia Street

White's Photo Gallery
See H. Wright.

Wiggin, Mrs. Agnes
(Royal Studio, Home Portrait Studio)
1911–1914: 610 Columbia Street
(Cunningham Block)
1914: 440 E. Columbia Street (Sapperton)
c. 1915–1918: 709 Columbia Street
(Westminster Trust Block)

Wright, H.
(White's [sic] Photo Gallery)
1905: 624 Columbia Street
(Hamley Block)

Chapter 1

1. Hill, p. 16–18.
2. Ireland, p. 85–107.
3. Hill, p. 43.
4. Woodland, p. 8.
5. Letters presented to the City of New Westminster by Queen Elizabeth II 1971, (New Westminster Museum and Archives Collection).
6. McLeod, p. 98.
7. Letter from Colonel R.C. Moody to Gov. James Douglas, March 17, 1859 (Provincial Archives Collection).
8. McLeod, p. 78–80.
9. Ormsby, p. 191.
10. McDonald, p. 435.

Chapter 2

1. *Mainland Guardian*, May 3, 1871, p. 3. "May Day."
2. B.C. Despatches, Seymour to Cardwell, March 14, 1865, p. 254.
3. *Mainland Guardian*, May 28, 1887, p. 3. "Great Guns."
4. *Mainland Guardian*, January 27, 1886, p. 3. "Briefs."
5. *The Province*, undated 1932 article, "He Grew Up with British Columbia," by R. Macey (New Westminster Museum and Archives Collection).
6. *Mainland Guardian*, April 10, 1886, p. 3. "An Angry Crowd."
7. *Mainland Guardian*, April 24, 1886, p. 3. "A Great Gathering."
8. *Mainland Guardian*, August 28, 1886, p. 3. "Our Branch."
9. *The Daily Columbian*, December 31, 1886, p. 3. "The Royal City."

Chapter 3

1. *The Truth*, December 31, 1890, p. 1. "Looking Backward."
2. *The Daily Columbian*, December 31, 1894, p. 1. "The Past Year."
3. *The Daily Columbian*, January 5, 1898, p. 1. "The Passing Year."

Chapter 4

1. *The Province*, September 12, 1898, p. 1. "Gone Up In A Hell of Roaring Flame."
2. *The Columbian*, September 17, 1898, p. 1. "Westminster's Big Fire."
3. *The Province*, September 12, 1898, p. 5. "Gone Up In A Hell of Roaring Flame."
4. *The Province*, September 24, 1898, p. 3. "New Westminster's Rise."

Chapter 5

1. *The Columbian Souvenir Exhibition Supplement*, October 4, 1899, p. 8. "Burned and Rebuilt."
2. *The Province*, October 5, 1898, p. 3. "New Westminster."
3. *The Columbian*, August 27, 1907, p. 1. "Moral Crusade … "
4. *The Daily Province*, August 5, 1905, p. 5. "Prosperity for the Royal City."
5. *The British Columbian Weekly*, August 5, 1913, p. 26. "Pictures of Typical Royal City Residences."
6. *The British Columbian Weekly*, January 14, 1913, p. 16. "Westminster Trust Building."
7. *The Vancouver Daily Province Anniversary Number*, February 15, 1913, p. 35. "New Westminster's Growing Time."

Chapter 6

1. *The British Columbian*, August 22, 1914, p. 1. "Soldiers Leave for the Front in Scene of Great Enthusiasm."
2. *The British Columbian Victory Edition*, June, 1919, "Home support to the Fighting Men."
3. *The British Columbian*, November 9, 1918, p. 5. "Epidemic is not over yet."
4. *The British Columbian*, November 8, 1918, p. 3. "Great News received with Unparalleled Enthusiasm."
5. *The British Columbian*, September 29, 1919, p. 1. "Thousands of City and Valley … "
6. *The British Columbian*, April 28, 1926, pp. 9–20. "Special Market Supplement."
7. *The British Columbian*, November 2, 1927, pp. 1–6. "Special Supplement."
8. *The British Columbian*, February 28, 1929, p. 10. "New Westminster Retains Reputation … "
9. *The British Columbian*, September 3, 1929, p. 1. "Fair Attendance Record is Broken."

Chapter 7

1. *The British Columbian*, July 17, 1935, p. 1. "Attempt to Burn Dockworkers Home."
2. *The British Columbian*, July 4, 1935, p. 1. "Fiery cross burned … "
3. *The British Columbian*, May 31, 1939, p. 1. "A Joyous Welcome."
4. *The British Columbian*, May 31, 1939, p. 1. "28 Elaborate Welcome Arches … "
5. The Royal Westminster Regiment website: http://www.army.dnd.ca/royal_westies/
6. *The British Columbian*, undated Clipping, "Westminster House Praised by Soldiers."
7. *The British Columbian*, December 9, 1941, p. 1. "Darkness Shrouds All City … "
8. *The British Columbian*, March 12, 1942, p. 1. "City Japanese Merchants Adopt Waiting Policy."
9. *The British Columbian*, May 7, 1945, p. 1. "News of Victory Greeted."
10. *The British Columbian*, January 21, 1946, p. 1. "City Rings with Mighty Cheers."

Chapter 8

1. *The Vancouver Sun*, May 3, 1955, p. 1. "New Westminster … "
2. Sanderson, p. 39.
3. *The British Columbian*, November 16, 1949, p. 12–13. "Eaton's Opens Fine New Store."
4. *The British Columbian*, November 21, 1950, p. 1. "Historic Centre Opened."
5. *The British Columbian*, November 20, 1953, p. 13. "Mayor and Ex-Mayors Open New City Hall."
6. Harker, p. 200.
7. *The Vancouver Sun*, May 5, 1960, p. 2B. "Sleeping Beauty Needs Awakening."
8. *The Vancouver Sun*, May 5, 1960, p. 1B. "New Westminster Royal by Any Standard."

Sidebars

Chapter 1: The Gentleman Photographer: Francis George Claudet 1837–1906

Mattison, "The Claudets of British Columbia," pp. 135–153.

Chapter 2: Judkins Floating Sunbeam Gallery: David R. Judkins 1836–1909

Mattison, *Camera Workers: The British Columbia Photographic Directory 1858–1900.*

Chapter 3: A Photographic Master: Stephen Joseph Thompson 1864–1929

"Our New Art Gallery," *The Daily Columbian,* October 28, 1886, p. 3.

Mattison, *Camera Workers …1858–1900.*

Chapter 4: Amateur Luck: Charles Ernest Bloomfield, 1877–1954

Bloomfield Family Collection, Additional Manuscript 973, Vancouver City Archives.

Tompson, John, nephew of C.E. Bloomfield. Personal interview. 1998.

Chapter 5: Through Japanese Eyes: Paul Louis Okamura, 1865–1937

Wolf, *The Portrait Studio of Paul Louis Okamura,* pp. 175–79.

Innoye, Myea, daughter of P.L. Okamura. Personal interview. 2004.

Chapter 6 : Pictorialist Partners: John Vanderpant, 1884–1939, Horace G. Cox, 1885–1972.

Arnold, *The Terminal City.*

Jeffries, *H.G. Cox.*

Salloum, *Underlying Vibrations.*

Hopkins, Susan, great-granddaughter of H.G. Cox. Personal interview. 2005.

Chapter 7: Pioneer Filmmaker: Hugh Norman Lidster 1888–1967.

Lidster, *Memories of Sixty Years.*

Springate, Nick, grandson of H.N. Lidster. Personal interview. 2005.

Chapter 8: The Tragedy of Stride Studios: Charles Edgar Stride, 1890–1972.

"How well do you know … C.E. Stride," *The British Columbian,* c. 1926, New Westminster Museum and Archives Collection.

"Charlie Stride Owns a Hatful of Records," *The British Columbian,* June 26, 1968, p .6.

"Man Missing in Royal City Fire," *The British Columbian,* December 23, 1968, p. 1.

"Lower Mainland will miss veteran city photographer," *The Columbian,* March 2, 1972, p. 3.

Kirkwood, D., former studio employee of C.E. Stride. Personal interview. 2005.

Books and Articles

Arnold, Grant. "The Terminal City and the Rhetoric of Utopia." From *Collapse #5*, "Rhetoric of Utopia: Early Modernism and the Canadian West Coast." Vancouver: Vancouver Art Gallery, 2000.

Ewert, Henry. *The Story of the B.C. Electric Railway Company.* North Vancouver: Whitecap Books, 1986.

Carlson, Keith T. et al., eds. *A Sto:lo–Coast Salish Historical Atlas.* Vancouver: Douglas & McIntyre, 2001.

Gresko, Jacqueline. "Roughing it in the Bush in British Columbia: Mary Moody's Pioneer Life in New Westminster 1858–1863." From B.K. Latham and R.J. Pazdro, *Not Just Pin Money: Selected Essays on the History of Women's Work in British Columbia.* Victoria: Camosun College, 1984.

Gresko, Jacqueline and Richard Howard. *Fraser Port: Freightway to the Pacific.* Victoria: Sono Nis Press, 1986.

Harker, Douglas E. *The Woodwards: The Story of a Distinguished British Columbia Family, 1850–1975.* Vancouver: Mitchell Press, 1976.

Harrison, Eli. "Public Commission of Inquiry into the Management of the Fire and Water Departments of the City of New Westminster, more especially with reference to the Fire which occurred on the 10th and the morning of the 11th of September 1898." Nanaimo: Province of British Columbia, 1899.

Hill, Beth. *Sappers: The Royal Engineers in British Columbia.* Ganges, BC: Horsdal & Schubart, 1987.

Ireland, Willard E. "First Impressions: Letter of Colonel Richard Clement Moody RE to Arthur Blackwood, Feb. 1, 1859." From *B.C. Historical Quarterly*, 15, 1951.

Jeffries, Bill. *H.G. Cox: British Columbia Pictorialist.* North Vancouver: Presentation House Gallery, 2004.

Lidster, H.N. *Memories of Sixty Years.* New Westminster: Unpublished memoir, 1964.

Mather, Barry and Margaret L.B. McDonald. *New Westminster: The Royal City.* Vancouver: J.M. Dent and Sons and the City of New Westminster, 1958.

Mattison, David. *Eyes of a City: Early Vancouver Photographers 1868–1900.* Occasional Paper No. 3. Vancouver: City of Vancouver Archives, 1986.

———. "The Claudets of British Columbia: Melting, Assaying and Photographing All Day." From *History of Photography: An International Journal*, vol. 14, no. 2 (April–June 1990).

———. *Camera Workers: The British Columbia Photographic Directory 1858–1900.* Victoria: Camera Workers Press, 1985.

———. *Camera Workers: The British Columbia Photographic Directory 1901–1950.* Victoria: David Mattison, 1996.

McDonald, Margaret L.B. *New Westminster 1859–1871.* Vancouver: University of British Columbia: Unpublished Master of Arts Thesis, 1947.

McLeod, Anne B. and Pixie McGeachie. *Land of Promise: Robert Burnaby's Letters from Colonial British Columbia 1858–1863.* Burnaby: City of Burnaby, 2002.

Moogk, Peter. *Vancouver Defended: A History of the Men and Guns of the Lower Mainland Defences 1859–1949.* Surrey: Antonson Publishing, 1978.

Ormsby, Margaret. *British Columbia: A History.* Vancouver: Macmillan, 1958.

Salloum, Sheryl. *Underlying Vibrations: The Photography and Life of John Vanderpant.* Vancouver: Horsdal & Schubart, 1995.

Sanderson, Eric. *Nature's Fury: The Inside Story to the Disastrous B.C. Floods.* Vancouver: Smith Publishing, 1948.

Wolf, Jim. "Second Port-City: An Overview of New Westminster Chinese Canadian Community." From *B.C. Historical News*, Vol. 21, No. 2, 1988.

———. "The Portrait Studio of Paul Louis Okamura." From *Shashin: Japanese Canadian Studio Photography to 1942.* An exhibition catalogue. Grace E. Thomson, ed. Burnaby: Japanese Canadian National Museum, 2005.

Woodland, Alan. *New Westminster: The Early Years 1858–1898.* New Westminster: Nunaga Publishing Company, 1973.

Woodward, Frances M. "The Influence of the Royal Engineers on the Development of British Columbia." From *B.C. Studies*, 24, 1974–75.

Newspapers

The British Columbian
The Columbian
The Daily Columbian
The Daily Province
The Province
The Mainland Guardian
The Truth
The Vancouver Daily Province
The Weekly Columbian

Archives

Provincial Archives of British Columbia
New Westminster Museum and Archives
Vancouver City Archives

INDEX

INDEX OF PHOTOGRAPHS